TIME IN LITERATURE

Time in Literature

BY HANS MEYERHOFF

UNIVERSITY OF CALIFORNIA PRESS
Berkeley and Los Angeles 1955

UNIVERSITY OF CALIFORNIA PRESS
Berkeley and Los Angeles
CAMBRIDGE UNIVERSITY PRESS
London, England
Copyright 1955 by
THE REGENTS OF THE UNIVERSITY OF CALIFORNIA
L. C. Catalogue Card No.: 55-5450
PRINTED IN THE UNITED STATES OF AMERICA
Designed by Rita Carroll

in memoriam
parentum

PREFACE

THIS study attempts to say something about certain significant aspects of time which seem to play a considerable part in literature and which seem to be excluded from the analysis of the concept of time in science.

A few personal words may be added, explaining how I came to be interested in this theme. It occurred to me originally about two years ago while attending a seminar given by my former colleague and friend, the late Hans Reichenbach. His lectures were based upon an analysis of the meaning of time in science—classical physics, thermodynamics, and quantum mechanics—and the application of time to certain related subjects like information theory. A book on this subject almost completed at the time of Mr. Reichenbach's death will be published posthumously.

I was then—as I have always been—interested in certain philosophical ideas in literature. Time is one of the ideas which have engaged literary minds throughout the ages and which have received special attention in contemporary literature. While listening to the lectures, I began to think about how remote the scientific, logical construction of the concept of time was from certain aspects of time in human experience which literature has often singled out for analysis. What seemed most significant in terms of the experience of time was quite irrelevant to the logical concept of time as formulated by science; per contra, the scientific concept seemed to have little to say about the most significant aspects of time in the lives of human beings. Startled by this striking contrast, I wondered why this was so, what the function of the literary analysis was as compared with the scientific analysis of time, why literature was so much concerned with this problem, particularly in our own age, and what, if anything, these questions had to do with philosophy. The following essay is the outcome of some of these reflections.

These comments will explain why the major part of this study (chapter ii) takes the form of a comparison between the literary and scientific treatment of time. I am, however, indebted to Mr. Reichenbach also for some of the content which I have put into this comparison. The little I know about the philosophy of science I have learned from him; and, as I have indicated, I have primarily drawn upon his writings for references in connection with the concept of time in nature. I wish to make it perfectly clear, however, that my comments on the construction of a physical theory of time are not meant to represent his views—nor meant as a serious analysis of the physical concept itself. (It is evident, therefore, that this study does not claim to be a systematic philosophical treatise on time in general.) I am using only a few, and what I believe to be generally accepted, ideas developed by a physical theory in order to approach and elaborate the entirely different aspects of time in experience and literature.

Conversely, this essay is not meant to be an exercise in literary criticism. I have used the data provided by literary works for the purpose of clarifying certain general aspects of time, not for the purpose of explaining their function in the specific works of writers cited. This may help also to bring out another important limitation of this study: In the works cited I am interested only in the treatment of time, not in other aspects which may, in effect, be more dominant and influential themes as far as the total structure of these works is concerned. Again, with regard to related problems discussed in the following pages, e.g., the self, mysticism, or mythology, it must be emphasized that I am considering only their possible connection with the subject of time, or the bearing of different views of time upon them. Save for this restriction, it would have been foolhardy to touch so briefly upon a number of extremely complex problems.

I realize, of course, that some people will consider the present project an impossible intellectual hybrid—neither science, nor literature, nor psychology, but an embarrassing mixture of all these disciplines. I have tried to deal with this problem in the last chapter which, from a philosophical point of view, is probably the most controversial. But whether or not my suggestions there are acceptable, it is worthwhile, I think, at least to attempt a borderline study and collect material from various intellectual disciplines, instead of succumbing to the fashion and/or necessity of increased specialization.

Aside from my personal interest in the subject, the only justification for this essay that I can think of is that I am not familiar with any work which deals with these problems. There are, of course, numerous studies, by various writers, on the concept of time or the aesthetic significance of literature as a temporal art; and I have tried to consult most of them. There are also numerous psychological studies of time; and I have tried to become familiar with them, too; but there is no work, so far as I know, which raises the philosophical problem of correlating the treatment of time in literature with aspects in experience and nature.

There are two works which deal with the problem of time in literature in a general, or philosophical, fashion: *Temps et Roman* by Jean Pouillon (Paris, 1946) and *Études Sur Le Temps Humain* by Georges Poulet (Paris, 1950; a second volume on the same theme, called *La Distance Intérieure*, appeared in 1952).

Pouillon's work is really not a book on time at all. It is chiefly concerned with the psychological and philosophical problem of the function of the imagination in literature. Only the second and smaller half of the book deals with *l'expression du temps;* but this expression of time is seen from a rather limited perspective of two existentialist categories: time viewed under the aspect of "contingency" (*les romans de la durée*) and time viewed under the aspect of fate (*les romans de la destinée*). This structure is quite insufficient for catching the variety of modes entering into the literary treatment of time.

Poulet's work, on the other hand, is a detailed study of time in human experience, but not a general or systematic one. The first volume deals with the concept of time in eighteen different writers, from Montaigne and Descartes to Valéry and Proust, and the second volume continues this piecemeal treatment. Poulet has collected important material, from numerous authors in post-Renaissance literature, which is indispensable for the subject of *le temps humain;* but the purpose and structure of his book are altogether different from those of the present study, which attempts a general interpretation of the treatment of time in literature in its relation to the self and the world of nature. In his introduction Poulet gives a historical survey of the development of the consciousness of time in the modern world, which I have found useful in connection with chapter iii below.

The notes indicate the other sources from which I have drawn. Permission was kindly granted me to quote longer passages from: *Remembrance of Things Past,* by Marcel Proust (New York: Random House, 1927), 2 vols.; *Proust: Portrait of a Genius,* by André Maurois (New York: Harper & Brothers, 1951); *The Great Gatsby,* by F. Scott Fitzgerald (New York: Charles Scribner's Sons, 1925; reprinted as a Bantam Book, 1945); *The Story of a Novel,* by Thomas Wolfe (New York: Charles Scribner's Sons, 1936; reprinted in the Signet Book edition, *Only the Dead Know Brooklyn,* 1947); and *New Introductory Lectures on Psychoanalysis,* by Sigmund Freud (New York: W. W. Norton & Co., Inc., 1933).

I regret that I did not see *Time and the Novel* by A. A. Mendilow (London: Peter Nevill, 1952) until the present essay was in print. Mr. Mendilow's book contains a great deal of excellent material which would have been helpful in corroborating and enlarging upon the literary evidence collected in the present volume. His analysis of the time structure of *Tristram Shandy* is particularly illuminating. His work differs from the present study in that Mr. Mendilow is primarily concerned with different perspectives of time in the total literary process—the temporal dimensions of the story, the characters, the writer, the reader, and their respective interactions—whereas I have tried to place the literary treatment of time in a more general philosophical and social framework. The fact that several critical studies on time in literature have now appeared, within the last few years, in widely different communities—Paris, Jerusalem, and Los Angeles—is another manifestation of the *Zeitgeist* on which I have ventured some comments in chapter iii below.

I am indebted to Mrs. Beatrice Novotny and Mrs. Ida Perry for generous help in typing the manuscript, and to Mr. Glenn Gosling and Mrs. Kathleen Leidich for their kind assistance in preparing the manuscript for the press. And I owe an expression of special thanks to two colleagues and friends, Maria Reichenbach and Ralph Cohen, for their interest and help, both personal and professional.

H. M.

University of California
Los Angeles, October, 1954.

CONTENTS

Chapter One

EXPERIENCE AND NATURE

TIME, as Kant and others have observed, is the most characteristic mode of our experience. It is more general than
space, because it applies to the inner world of impressions,
emotions, and ideas for which no spatial order can be given.
It is also more directly and immediately given than space or
any other general concept such as causality or substance.
The blooming, buzzing confusion of experience seems to
convey an immediate awareness that certain elements succeed each other, change, or endure. Succession, flux, change,
therefore, seem to belong to the most immediate and primitive data of our experience; and they are aspects of time.
There is no experience, as it were, which does not have a
temporal index attached to it.

Time is particularly significant to man because it is inseparable from the concept of the self. We are conscious of
our own organic and psychological growth in time. What

we call the self, person, or individual is experienced and known only against the background of the succession of temporal moments and changes constituting his biography. But how can that which constantly changes be called the same person or an identical self? How can man be "for himself" if he always experiences himself as different and if he is always known as different from moment to moment in time? What is man, if he is nothing but a victim of temporal succession and change? What, if anything, endures throughout the constantly changing stream of consciousness of the individual? The question, what is man, therefore invariably refers to the question of what is time. The quest for a clarification of the self leads to a *recherche du temps perdu*. And the more seriously human beings become engaged in this quest, the more they become preoccupied and concerned with the consciousness of time and its meaning for human life.

A temporal index enters into the self-consciousness of man as well as into the study of man and society. "Organic life exists only insofar as it evolves in time. . . . We cannot describe the momentary state of an organism without taking its history into consideration and without referring it to a future state for which this state is merely a point of passage." [1] Cassirer's words only reëcho what was the major thesis of the historical, evolutionary, and organic theories developed during the nineteenth century. From Hegel to Marx, from Comte to Darwin, from Bergson to Whitehead, these theories selected the temporal element as a basic methodological or metaphysical principle. Thus Hegel formulated a new, "dialectical," logic the basic categories of which were designed to catch temporal change and dynamic interaction of events in a formalized system. Marx, Comte, and Darwin introduced temporal "laws" into history, sociology, and biology; Freud, into psychology.

"Historicism," defined as a temporal, evolutionary, or genetic mode of explanation, came to be recognized as the most characteristic method for the study of man and society.[2] It has now become an integral part of the general climate of opinion. The modern mind is deeply conscious of time as a universal condition of life and as an ineradicable factor in our knowledge of man and society. The meaning of this increasing preoccupation with time in the modern world will be examined in chapter iii below.

This emergence of time into the foreground of modern consciousness is also reflected in literature. Literature—like music—is a temporal art; "for time is the medium of narration, as it is the medium of life."[3] And "once upon a time" is the "timeless" theme of every story told by man, from fairy tales to the opening sentence of the *Portrait of the Artist as a Young Man*. To be engaged in literature, therefore, quite naturally leads to questions about the meaning of time for the art form itself. Moreover, if art holds a mirror up to human nature, and if man is more conscious than he was of the pervasive and precarious nature of time, then this consciousness will be reflected increasingly in literary works.

This is borne out in the writing of our own age. Time has become, as Wyndham Lewis was perhaps the first to point out,[4] an over-all and predominant theme in recent literature. Perhaps this literature has even cultivated so morbid a sense of time as to justify Mr. Lewis' hysterical protest against it. But time has always been in and on men's minds. What has happened in our age is only a difference in the degree to which this preoccupation with time has become explicit and articulate—especially in conjunction with the problem of man; and this for a good reason, as I shall try to show later.

It would be useless to document this preëminent position of time in contemporary literature. Aside from the writers whose contributions we shall consider below, there is hardly a major figure in recent literature who has not raised the problem of time and its relation to man; and the theme recurs so frequently in popular works that the titles alone referring to "time," must, I suspect, run into the hundreds or thousands.

I propose to discuss some general aspects of the problem of time in literature, especially in recent literature. More specifically, I am interested in the following questions: (1) What is meant by "time" in literature? (2) What are the major elements of time in literature? (3) What is the meaning of time in the modern world; or why is time such a prominent theme in contemporary literature? (4) What is the significance of this literary treatment of time for philosophy? The key questions are those referring to the major aspects of time in literature and to the causes responsible for the rise of time in the modern world.

* * *

Time in literature always refers to elements of time as given in experience. What these elements are I shall try to show in the following chapter. Here I wish to make a few preliminary remarks about the distinction between time in experience and time in nature.

Time in literature is *le temps humain,* the consciousness of time as it is part of the vague background of experience or as it enters into the texture of human lives. Its meaning, therefore, is to be sought only within the context of this world of experience or within the context of a human life as the sum total of these experiences. Time so defined is private, personal, subjective or, as is often said, psychological. These terms mean that we are thinking of time as directly and immediately experienced.

There is, of course, another way of thinking about time, which is also quite familiar. This is to construct a concept of time which is not private, subjective, or defined in terms of experience, but which is public, objective, or defined in terms of "the objective structure of the time relation" in nature.[5] This is the concept of time in physics, expressed by the symbol "t" in mathematical equations. It is also our "public" time, which we use, with the aid of watches, calendars, etc., in order to synchronize our private experiences of time for the purpose of social action and communication. Characteristics of this concept of time are that it is independent of how we personally experience time, that it has intersubjective validity, and, most importantly, that it is believed to refer to an objective structure in nature rather than to a subjective background of human experience.

This familiar distinction is pertinent to our subsequent discussion for the following reason: The notion of time "given as an immediate datum of our consciousness" (Bergson), apparently a simple and indubitable fact of everybody's experience, turns out to be highly ambiguous and unreliable when used for the purpose of constructing a scientific concept of time applicable to an objective structure of nature. What is psychologically simple and directly given is by no means logically clear and valid. In fact, a long and elaborate process of rational abstraction, construction, and interpretation is needed in order to make the transition from the notion of time as given in experience to an "axiomatic system" of time believed to be objectively valid in nature.

Yet the scientific analysis, objectively valid as it is, turns out to be quite estranged from the subjective experience of time. Thus what is logically clear and valid seems to be psychologically false and meaningless. So wide is the gap between these two notions of time that each seems to be quite irrelevant to the other, although the scientist also starts from and is familiar with the subjective experience of time, and although we are all familiar with and dependent upon the objective concept of time constructed by the scientist.

It is this dilemma, or apparent paradox between time as an immediate datum of consciousness and time as a logical construct claiming objective validity, which sets the general frame of reference for any inquiry into the meaning of time and poses puzzling questions for scientific and philosophical analysis. Nowhere, perhaps, is this dichotomy between the world of experience and the world of scientific concepts more striking than in the case of time—precisely because time as experienced has such crucial significance for human life in general and because the scientific analysis of time seems to disregard this significant connection.

The difficulty of making the transition from what is psychologically simple and immediately given to what is logically clear and objectively valid in nature has frequently been emphasized by writers on the subject of time. This is what St. Augustine had in mind in the most famous and most often quoted formulation of the dilemma: "What, then, is time? If no one asks of me, I know; if I wish to explain to him who asks, I know not." [6] Or as a writer in the seventeenth century expressed it: "I lose thee while I seek to find thee out." [7] "A few questions [about time]," Russell wrote recently, "can reduce [us] to hopeless confusion." As an illustration he adds a brief dialogue by which a clever dialectician can induce this state of confusion in the minds of those of us who approach the problem of time in terms of experience or common sense. "Does the past exist? No. Does the future exist? No. Then only the present exists. Yes. But within the present there is no lapse of time? Quite so. Then time does not exist? Oh, I wish you wouldn't be so tiresome." [8] This is, of course, only a restatement of the ancient puzzle which Zeno, a clever Eleatic dialectician, propounded in order to prove that time was unreal. Whatever happens, happens *now;* but "now" does not include change, motion, or lapse of time. Thus the arrow, in its flight through space and time, is, at any given moment or "now," always standing still—which seems to make mockery of our common-sense notions of flying through space and time.

When we try to go beyond the content of our immediate experience or common-sense notions of time, we seem to be "lost and embrangled in inextricable difficulties," as Berkeley said [9]—whether it is a matter of defining some of the basic concepts, such as lapse, interval, moment, order, direction, which are indispensable in clarifying what we mean by past, present, and future; or whether it is a matter of comparing our views of time with those held by peoples in primitive cultures.[10] There is ample evidence on both these points throughout the voluminous literature on time.

In fact, the difficulties encountered in proceeding from the fact of time in experience to a logically sound theory of time are so perplexing and overwhelming that many thinkers, from Zeno to Bradley, concluded that the whole subject of time was riddled with contradictions which could never be resolved; hence, that time was not a rational concept. And since it was believed that "reality" must be rational, it followed that time was declared to be unreal and illusory, that is, not an aspect of any objective part of reality whatsoever. Reality, according to this view, was without or beyond time, timeless and unchanging.

Thus what at first seems the most immediate datum of

experience becomes, as a result of this kind of analysis, a meaningless illusion. There is no longer any connection between the world of "appearance" (i.e., experience) and the world of "reality" as far as the category of time and its meaning in human lives are concerned. And we might well wonder why something so frightfully real in terms of our own experiences and lives should be declared an illusion because it doesn't fit the shoe of some special system of logic; or as Boodin put it, "calling a thing an illusion doesn't free us from the responsibility of accounting for how an eternal, static system could produce the illusion or appearance."[11]

St. Augustine was the first thinker to advance an ingenious philosophical theory based entirely upon the momentary experience of time combined with the psychological categories of memory and expectation. What happens, happens *now*, he argued; that is, it is always an experience, idea, or thing which is "present." Nevertheless, we can construct a meaningful temporal series accounting for past and future in terms of memory and expectation. By "past" we then mean the present memory experience of a thing past; by "future," the present expectation or anticipation of a future thing.[12]

This important and highly influential theory about time in terms of experience was reëchoed in the seventeenth and eighteenth centuries by Hobbes, Locke, Condillac, Berkeley, and Hume. The strength of this theory lies in its roots within human experience; its weakness, in the openly subjective nature of the theory. The past—even the past of our own lives —must have a different nature or status from our recollections of it. We generally assume that there is "an objective time-order of events to which my recollections refer"[13] and not that recollections are the *only* justification for ordering events in time. This is impressed on us still more forcibly when we think of the past as applied to nature in general: the origin and evolution of the universe, the records of astronomical and geological time beyond the reach of any human experience, or the past of man's own evolution and history; all these, we assume, exhibit characteristics of succession, change, order, and direction which are quite objective, i.e., independent of our experience of time.

It appears necessary, therefore, even from the point of view of common sense, to construct a theory of time which will satisfy these conditions. The objective of a scientific theory, therefore, is to eliminate the ambiguities and perplexities of subjective experience. Unfortunately, this process of constructing an axiomatic system of time believed to be objectively valid in nature also eliminates certain *qualities* of time which are charged with great *significance* in human experience.

This is the dilemma posed by the apparent irreconcilability of time in experience and time in nature. The irreconcilable elements contained in these two dimensions of time are, I believe, the chief reason for the divergent philosophical interpretations of time. These interpretations are invariably conditioned by the fact that they deal (or attempt to deal) either with time in experience or with time in nature. The need for a scientific, axiomatic system of time is to be found in the ambiguities and perplexities of time in experience. The axiomatic, logical system, however, is achieved only at the expense of neglecting or eliminating certain qualities of time which are extremely significant within the world of man's experience. This is the reason, I think, that there have been, throughout the history of thought, numerous and repeated attempts to clarify the meaning of those components of time which are an integral part of human life but not a part of any scientific theory.

Literature and what I shall call "literary types" of philosophy are attempts of this kind. "It was the analysis of the notion of time," Bergson wrote in a letter to William James, "as that enters into mechanics and physics, which overturned all my ideas. I saw, to my great astonishment, that scientific time does not *endure* . . . that positive science consists essentially in the elimination of duration. This was the point of departure for a series of reflections which brought me, by gradual steps, to reject almost all of what I had hitherto accepted and to change my point of view completely." [14] Bergson, of course, was thinking of time as an "immediate datum of consciousness," and the theory he constructed makes sense only within this frame of reference. Yet it is easy to understand why Bergson's philosophy has exercised so profound an influence on literature: the literary treatment of time, as we shall see, has always been "Bergsonian" in the sense of analyzing time as an immediate datum of consciousness and as it enters into human lives and actions rather than "into mechanics and physics."

These introductory remarks serve as the point of departure for the general problem. The contrast between the two notions of time—in experience and in nature—will now be developed in detail by showing what the major aspects of time are, as they occur in literature or in literary types of philosophy, and how these elements of time are related to the world of human experience and existence.

Chapter Two

ASPECTS OF TIME IN LITERATURE

I NOW pass to an examination of the major elements of time as they are treated in literary works or literary types of philosophy in contrast to the scientific analysis of the concept of time. These elements, as we said, invariably refer to certain *qualities* which are significant in experience and in the lives of human beings and which are inadequately rendered by or altogether omitted from a scientific theory. The following comments on the physical theory of time are meant to serve as a general background in order to clarify, by comparison and contrast, the structure of time as disclosed by literature.

An axiomatic system of time in nature involves the clarification of at least three major concepts: (1) measurement (or metric); (2) order; and (3) direction.[1] Objective criteria must be worked out for these concepts so that we are able to say that they are valid for a time series in nature independently of the subjective experiences of human beings. These criteria must coördinate a set of definitions with processes in nature rather than with processes inside human beings. To devise such coördinative definitions for the meaning of an objective metric, order, and direction of time in nature has been the work of scientists, scientific philosophers, and logicians. These concepts, as we shall see, find an altogether different expression within the context of experience and literature.

Subjective Relativity

Measurement, or the metric of time, involves comparatively simple considerations. We all know that our own experiences are a poor basis for measuring time objectively. Now it goes fast; now it goes slowly; now we are keenly conscious of every second ticking off; now we seem completely oblivious to or unconscious of the passage of time. These subjective irregularities, lapses, and misjudgments indicate the need for objective criteria for the measuring of time. Throughout the history of science, our basic units of measurement were believed to be objective when they were coördinated with certain objects in nature for which a measurable uniform standard of motion could be determined. Sometimes these objects have been the earth and the moon— "lunar time"; sometimes, the earth and the sun—"solar time"; the astronomer has now chosen as the basis for an objective metric of time the rotation of the earth with reference to the system of fixed stars—"sidereal time." This is the most (though not perfectly) uniform standard of measurement, and by it we set our clocks and calendars. It is also completely objective in the sense of referring to motions the uniformity of which is independent of human experience.

Only the kind of motion selected for measurement may be said to be arbitrary or conventional; the motions themselves are not. They are part of nature independent of man.

Such a metric of time is absolutely indispensable for the practical purposes of action and communication. Without it we would be lost in a sea of subjective relativity. Nevertheless, however indispensable for a wide range of activity, this analysis immediately sets up a sharp cleavage between the scientific concept of time and some of the most familiar and trivial elements of time in experience. Insofar as we stay within the domain of personal experience, there is an arbitrary, unreal quality about the objective measurement of time set by the sidereal clocks and calendars. In practical affairs we are constantly part of an objective time order measured quantitatively and uniformly according to the behavior of objects in nature; at the same "time," we are also conscious that these events have an entirely different quality in that they are part of the subjective time order of personal experience.

Time as experienced exhibits the quality of subjective relativity, or is characterized by some sort of unequal distribution, irregularity, and nonuniformity in the personal metric of time. This quality differs radically from the regular, uniform, quantitative units characteristic of an objective metric. This phenomenon—quite commonplace and familiar —has been extensively reported in scientific psychological literature, where the organic and psychological conditions responsible for this subjective relativity have been widely studied and interpreted. It is not my purpose to review or comment upon these studies, but merely to show briefly that the same phenomenon has also been a frequent source of wonderment in literature: "When it seems long to you, then it *is* long; when it seems short, why, then, it is short. But

how long, or how short it actually is, that nobody knows."
Or: "To be susceptible of being measured, time must flow
evenly, but who ever said it did that? As far as our consciousness is concerned, it doesn't, we only assume it does for
the sake of convenience; and our units of measurement are
purely arbitrary, sheer conventions." [2] Proust records the
same phenomenon: "The time that is ours to use each day is
elastic: the passions we feel dilate it, those that we inspire
contract it, and habit fills it." [3] Again, in the words of Virginia Woolf: "The mind of man works with strangeness
upon the body of time. An hour, once it lodges in the queer
element of the human spirit, may be stretched to fifty or a
hundred times its clock length; on the other hand, an hour
may be accurately represented by the timepiece of the mind
by one second." [4] These references, which could be multi-
plied ad libitum, may suffice to call attention to the quality
of subjective relativity in the personal metric of time as
treated in some contemporary works. The conflict between
this subjective metric and the objective metric of clocks is
perfectly familiar from common-sense observations and from
psychological tests. Besides, it is by no means the most significant aspect of time in experience.

Of Time and the River

Much more significant is another phenomenon, the aspect
of duration. I am using Bergson's term because it was for
him the point of departure for a theory constructed in articulate opposition to the physical concept of time and because
this theory has made him a very influential thinker so far as
modern literature is concerned. Duration simply means that
we experience time as a continuous flow. The experience of
time is characterized not only by successive moments and

multiple changes but also by something which endures within succession and change. It was Bergson's contention, reëchoed in the literary treatment of time, that this quality of continuous flow or duration does not find an adequate correlate in the physical concept of time.

Physics, according to this view, translates time into the dimension of space; the intellect "spatializes" time, as Bergson said, by which he meant that the quality of continuous flow, duration, and "unity within multiplicity," characteristic of the experience of time, is converted, by the physical theory, into separate, distinct, measurable quantities which always remain separate, disparate, and unrelated, like points in space or marks on a chronometer. It is this contrast—or the neglect of duration—which caused him to speak of physical time as a distortion or falsification of the "essential nature" of time. This is a permissible mode of speech if used to emphasize the difference between certain qualitative aspects of experience and certain quantitative aspects of time in nature. Otherwise it obviously ignores the question of what is "essential" about time, especially since the personal, subjective components are inadequate for the construction of an objective theory.

Zeno used this dilemma in order to deny the reality of time; and the same dilemma has often figured prominently in philosophical literature. Kant, as we shall see, was concerned, long before Bergson, with the question of how the qualities of continuity and unity could arise out of the temporal succession of discontinuous, disparate events; e.g., the "duration" supervening upon the succession of separate sounds of the clock striking the hour. In fact, about the time Bergson launched his attack upon physical time as a distortion of time in experience, the mathematical theory of continuity and infinity as developed by Cantor, Russell, and others resolved

Bergson's dilemma and Zeno's paradoxes by giving a precise logical reconstruction of the experiential properties of duration, flow, or continuous change and motion.[5] There is no evidence that Bergson ever took account, or considered the adequacy, of this logical theory.

Literature does not deal with this, or any other, problem on the level of abstract theory. Nevertheless, the quality of continuous flow or duration has been an ageless theme in literary works from Ecclesiastes and Heraclitus to Joyce, Eliot, and Thomas Wolfe. The most familiar literary notation for making this quality explicit is the symbolism of the "river" and the "sea," or the sensible images of "flight" and "flowing." [6]

> "In the same river, we both step and do not step, we are and we are not."
>
> "One thing at least is certain—this life flies."
>
> "Time is like a river." "Of time and the river." "And time still passing . . . like a leaf . . . fading like a flower . . . time passing like a river flowing." "The river is within us, the sea is all about us." "Every man on earth holds in the little tenement of his flesh and spirit the whole ocean of human life and time."
>
> "Riverrun, past Eve and Adam's." "Beside the rivering waters of, hithering and thithering waters of."
>
> "Life is like a river, and as fixed, unutterable in unceasing movement and in changeless change as the great river is, and time itself."

The metaphor of the "stream" as attached to consciousness has become a symbol for a literary technique. "Stream of consciousness" signifies what the symbolism of time and the river has always meant to convey, namely, that time as experienced has the quality of "flowing," and that this quality is an enduring element within the constantly changing and successive moments of time. The quality of duration is superimposed, as it were, upon continuous change. Literature has played upon these themes abundantly and repetitiously throughout the ages. Wolfe's expression of "changeless change," for example, or Bergson's discovery of duration itself, was anticipated by Goethe's "duration within change" in the poem bearing this title.[7] But this is not the only kind of literary symbolism employed to convey the notion of duration. In the following passage by Virginia Woolf, for example, duration is actually projected into the world of things: ". . . there is a coherence in things, a stability; something, she meant, is immune from change, and shines out (she glanced at the window with its ripple of reflected light) in the face of the flowing, the fleeting, the spectral, like a ruby; so that again tonight she had the feeling she had had once today, already, of peace, of rest. Of such moments, she thought, the thing is made that endures." [8] Thomas Wolfe describes a similar vision from the window of a train that was passing a woman standing in a doorway: "Fixed in no-time, the slattern vanished, fixed, without a moment of transition." [9] Again, "no-time" is the moment that endures. That this repetition has not made the theme shopworn indicates how familiar and striking this phenomenon must be in human experience.

From a psychological point of view, continuous flow and duration are often said to constitute the experience of the "specious present." This is only another term introduced in order to describe the aspect of breadth, extension, or duration of the momentary experience of time as against the single, abstract point defining the moment of physical time. The "specious present," however, is also used to suggest that the flow of time within the present already contains some primitive elements of order and direction pointing toward "past" and "future." The present, as William James said (influenced by Bergson), has "a certain breadth of its own on which we sit perched and from which we look in two directions into time." [10] What James meant was that the temporal stretch enduring throughout the present includes elements from memory and expectation, and that these elements, remembered and anticipated, coalescing in the experience of the specious present, suggest to us some vague notions of "before" and "after," "earlier" and "later," "past" and "future" —terms which refer to the order and direction of time. It is these divisions in terms of memory and expectation which, as we saw, were singled out by St. Augustine as the key for a philosophical theory of time entirely based on experience.

Order and Association

Memory and expectation, therefore, seem to introduce a primitive basis for distinguishing between events which are called "earlier" (i.e., past) and events which are called "later" (i.e., future), even within the specious present. But these distinctions will not do for an *objective* ordering of the time-series into past and future. They do not satisfy the requirement, generally endorsed by common sense and indispensable for a scientific theory, that there is a temporal series of events in nature and history which is independent of our subjective experiences and to which our recollections and anticipations may or may not correspond. Moreover, memory and expectation are proverbially vague, ambiguous, and fallible. They are vague in that they often fuse and overlap even in the present; and they are fallible, or a constant source of error and deception, because of a number of psychological mechanisms—such as forgetting, repressing, distorting, or projecting. These effects, again, have been frequently studied in psychological literature.

The concept of the order of time may be given an objective meaning when it is coördinated with the principle of causality. Kant did this in his famous justification of the principle of causality. In response to Hume's skepticism, Kant tried to show that causality was indispensable for an objective ordering of events in time. What we mean by saying that A is "earlier" than B, speaking objectively, i.e., independently of the way we experience or remember the sequence of events, is that we can construct a causal relationship between the two events. If A is the cause of B, then A must be "earlier" than B; A must "precede" B; or A belongs to the past, B to the future. Only by presupposing the principle of causality, therefore, can we distinguish between an objective and subjective ordering of temporal sequences in the world; and since this distinction, in turn, is presupposed in all our knowledge about nature, Kant concluded that causality itself must be an objective principle in nature. Whether or not this conclusion was justified is of no concern to us here.

The use of the causal principle for a definition of an objective order of time is seen most easily in the so-called irreversible processes of nature; e.g., running a film backward or unscrambling eggs.[11] What is so "weird" about these sequences is that the relationship of cause and effect is violated; that is, stirring eggs causes them to be scrambled, not vice versa; hence we say the time order is wrong and distorted; past and future are reversed. It happens to be an empirical fact of this world that cause and effect define this unique serial order of time; if they didn't, we couldn't give this empirical, objective interpretation to the notions of "earlier" and "later" or to the concepts of past and future.

Strictly speaking, the irreversible processes just mentioned define not only the order but also the direction of time. Order alone is an asymmetrical relation determined by cause and effect, even if we do not know that this relation is irreversible. Given A as the cause and B as the effect, this relation establishes an order of "earlier" and "later," "past" and "future" without any reference to the ultimate direction of this temporal sequence. Irreversible processes, however, like scrambling eggs, are much stronger; they define a unidirectional causal order. In other words, they add to the concept of order the notion that the sequence of "earlier" and "later," "past" and "future" proceeds in one direction only.

Another empirical criterion may be used for distinguishing between past and future.[12] It also happens to be an empirical fact about the world—including our own minds—that the past leaves traces, marks, or records, and the future does not. Thus we say that an event was "earlier," or belongs to the order of the past, if it left a trace, mark, or record; events which have not yet left a record belong to the future. By past we then mean the entire collection of recorded history—whether of the universe or of man; by future that which does not have a history. Traces and records of the past may be natural or man made. Thus we leave records or inscribe marks so as to orient ourselves with regard to an objective order of time as against the vague and fallible order of events in memory.

The human mind is also a "recording instrument" like the earth (geological records) or the tools and instruments of man (archaeological records); and what we call memory is a repository or reservoir of records, traces, and engrams of past events analogous to the records preserved in geological strata.[13] There is no memory of the future. It is only by virtue of this empirical fact that memory serves as the subjective basis for the past as experienced. Strictly speaking, this fact is a consequence of the causal theory for an objective time order; for wherever we find traces—whether footprints in the sand, fingerprints on a gun, or faces indelibly imprinted in memory—we assume that these records were caused by events *preceding* them, and are not the result of events coming later.

Now it is perfectly obvious that these empirical facts deeply permeate our lives. Being invited to go to a party, or recording and remembering this fact, we say comes "before" our actual going to the party, because the former is the cause of the latter. It would never occur to anybody to think that our going to the party, i.e., the future, was the cause of the telephone call that invited us, i.e., the past; hence, it would never occur to anybody, in this context, to doubt the causal criterion for an objective ordering of temporal events. For all practical purposes, therefore, we recognize an objective time order as defined by the principle of causality, just as we recognize, for all practical purposes, an objective standard of measurement in terms of sidereal time. Time in nature consists not only of quantitative, uniform units of measurement but also of a *uniform series* or *linear order* in terms of cause and effect. There are, as is sometimes said, no closed causal chains in nature.

Although the causal principle prevails in the temporal order of nature, and although the human body and mind are an integral part of this physical order, the records stored in our memories pose special questions and difficulties; and these have often been explored by literary works. Memory is a much more complicated and confusing recording instrument than nature, man-made tools, or historical records. Its complexity and confusion arise from the fact that, instead of a uniform serial order, memory relations exhibit a *nonuniform, dynamic order* of events. Things remembered are fused and confused with things feared and hoped for. Wishes and fantasies may not only be remembered as facts, but the facts remembered are constantly modified, reinterpreted, and relived in the light of present exigencies, past fears, and future hopes.

The objective order of temporal sequences, therefore, forms only a partial, though indispensable, aspect of our memory structure; it is an order partial, as it were, to the world of clocks, dates, and physical records. A major portion of the contents of our memory does not exhibit this kind of uniform, serial order but rather a quality by which past, present, and future events are dynamically fused and associated with each other. This does not mean, of course, that the principle of causality does not hold for the contents of our memory. On the contrary, we say that feelings of pride, shame, fear, and love, or objects of dreams and imagination, *cause* the confusion and distortion of things remembered. Moreover, the principle of association within the private world of inner experience presupposes the principle of causality as much as does the connection between physical events in nature. Causality, therefore, prevails in the inner world as much as in the outer; but the causal connections (or associations) between events within memory do not constitute an objective, uniform, consecutive order of "earlier" and "later" as they do for events in nature. Instead they exhibit, as Bergson said, a quality of "dynamic interpenetration." It is this quality which is particularly significant for the relationship between time and the self.

This characteristic of time in memory may be expressed more precisely: The quality of dynamic interpenetration of events in memory manifests itself in a temporal sequence which is quite orderly. Events remembered, however much distorted and disordered they may be when viewed from an objective historical frame of reference, do follow each other, according to the causal principle, in an orderly manner; that is, event A follows event B, etc. The point, therefore, is that this peculiar order of the inner life appears as, or must be judged as, a form of disorder when it is compared with an objective temporal sequence. In contrast to the latter, the order of events in memory exhibits the quality of dynamic association and interpenetration.

This characteristic order—or disorder—of time in human lives has become a central point in the literary "analysis" of time and in philosophical theories, like Bergson's, that have taken the same phenomenon as their point of departure. The literary notation for this phenomenon is the "logic of images." This is the "logic" behind the method of free association and the interior monologue.

The logic of images is a familiar device in literature, especially in poetry. The term "logic" is, of course, a misnomer, for this logic is distinguished by the fact that its causal connections are altogether different—i.e., "illogical"—from those in ordinary logic, by which is meant either the logic of common sense or the logic of inductive, causal inferences defining objective sequences and connections in the external world. Instead, the logic of images or association is an attempt to show that, so far as the temporal sequences and *order* of events within the inner world of experience and memory are concerned, we must employ symbols of *disorder* that violate the strictly "logical" order and progression of events to which we have become accustomed by science and common sense. We must do so because the inner world of experience and memory exhibits a structure which is causally determined by *significant associations* rather than by objective causal connections in the outside world. To render this peculiar structure, therefore, requires a symbolism or imagery in which the different modalities of time—past, present, and future—are not serially, progressively, and uniformly ordered but are always inextricably and dynamically associated and mixed up with each other.

The logic of images is not a discovery of contemporary literature; it is impossible to approach any literary work without using this device as a clue to its structure, order, and "meaning." What is characteristic of modern literature is its development of an elaborate and intricate technique of "association"—or "free association" as it is sometimes called, after the psychoanalytic term to which it is related, but from which it differs—for rendering this logic of images. "I love that word 'association'; for me, and in however relative a sense, that which is full of associations is quite precisely that which is significant." [14]

Significance, according to this statement by Thomas Mann, is a function of the quality of the dynamic association of events in experience. Or, it is by association that the sequences of events in human experience are charged with value and disvalue. Significance, then, refers to a value-charged aspect of experience, "in however relative a sense." It is in this sense that I have used the term throughout this study. This sense of significance, therefore, is to be distinguished from the term "meaning" in the objective, logical sense. It is, to use a different terminology, not a cognitive, but a value-charged sense of "meaning"; and literature and the arts have always predominantly dealt with this kind of meaning in the sense of significance. Again, it would be supererogatory to cite any specific evidence for the role which the associative technique has played in modern literature. In the poetry of the symbolists and imagists, in the stream of consciousness of the novel, the dynamic fusion of temporal elements is one of the most pervasive and striking characteristics of modern literature. "The interior monologue appears as the real novel of time." [15] And instances of this kind abound in contemporary prose: in Proust and Valéry, in Joyce and Virginia Woolf, in Doeblin and Hermann Hesse, in Dos Passos and Faulkner.

I wish to consider briefly an extreme development of this trend. The qualities of continuous flow, duration, and dynamic association are most vivid in sleep, dreams, and fantasies—the most subjective experiences possible. Insofar as modern literature, like modern culture in general, has become particularly time-conscious, it has often chosen these states of the self as a key to making these aspects of time explicit and articulate. While going to sleep, as in the beginning of *Swann's Way*; in dreams and fantasies, as in *Finnegan's Wake*; and in normal or drug-induced states of hallucination, as in *The Confessions of an Opium Eater* or *Kubla Khan*, there is the purest experience of duration as well as of the dynamic fusion of all the elements ordinarily divided according to an objective order of time. There is a continuous flow and a complete intermixture of "before" and "after" or past and future suspending these objective categories and, strange as it may be to ordinary logic, encompassing all the events of one night or the accumulated store of experience constituting one lifetime, even extending beyond the frontiers of individual experience and memory to "enduring" aspects of the life of mankind. As De Quincey confessed under the influence of drugs: "The sense of space and, in the end, the sense of time were both powerfully affected. . . . Sometimes, I seemed to have lived a hundred years in one night; nay sometimes had feelings of a *duration* far beyond the limits of any human experience." [16] De Quincey's record corresponds closely to the enormous extension and condensation of time achieved in works like *Mrs Dalloway* or *Finnegan's Wake*. One day or night stretches into a lifetime and beyond. If such a temporal perspective is introduced, departing so radically from any objective metric and order, it is not difficult to take another step and say that the ordinary modalities of time—past, present, and future—are, strictly speaking, indistinguishable in experience; that they are contained (even those not actually experienced) as infinite possibilities within *any* moment of the life span of an individual; or that they may be viewed under the aspect of a timeless co-presence. Then it is possible to say, as Wolfe did, that we "shall see begin in Crete four thousand years ago the love that ended yesterday in Texas." This peculiar notion of a "timeless" co-presence of temporal elements in fantasy and imagination will be considered later.

Again, it is not only the modern or "surrealist" writer—Baudelaire, Rimbaud, Strindberg, Schnitzler, Joyce, Cocteau and others—who chooses to write dream poetry, novels, and plays. It is only that these themes have become more frequent in recent literature than they were in the past. Dreams and fantasies are experiences particularly suitable for conveying both the quality of duration and the quality of dynamic disorder and association. Characteristically enough, these are aspects of experience farthest removed from the data relevant to the construction of an objective theory of time and to the practical pursuits of life. The dream symbolism itself is as old as *The Sleeping Beauty*. The fairy tale, however, also expresses quite a different aspect of time; for the sleeping beauty is awakened from timeless sleep and immortal beauty to return to the world of time and mortality.

Of Time and the Self

Goethe called his remembrances of things past *Poetry and Truth* (*Dichtung und Wahrheit*). The title indicates that the literary reconstruction of one's life invariably involves two dimensions: a subjective pattern of significant associations (poetry) and an objective structure of verifiable biographical and historical events (truth). Both dimensions are present, not only in biographical and autobiographical forms of literature, but in any literary portrait whatsoever. There is no way of constructing a man's life, whether real or fictional, except through reconstructing his past in terms of significant associations supervening upon the objective, historical data, or except through showing the inseparable intermixture of the two dimensions. What may be called a "literary reconstruction" of man has always used, in addition to the objective, historical data, the pattern of significant associations in the stream of consciousness and in memory as the most important clue to the structure of the personality or the identity of the self.

The problem of time in experience, therefore, has its most interesting implications in conjunction with the problem of man. "Time is the medium of narration as it is the medium of life." We must now try to show how some of the qualities of time, which we have just worked out, acquire special significance in connection with the literary portrait of man.

At this point the literary treatment of time and the self merges imperceptibly with what I have called "literary types" of philosophy. Man may not have a nature, but he certainly has a history, as Dilthey said. Thus time, or the historical aspect of human existence, has become the focal point for an "existentialist" analysis of man. Time, according to Heidegger, is the basic category of existence[17]—time as it is experienced by the individual himself, not as it is recorded by the natural scientist or by the historian. Time is charged with "significance" for man because human life is lived under the shadow of time, because the question, what *am* I, makes sense only in terms of what I have *become*, that is, in terms of the objective historical facts together with the pattern of significant associations constituting the biography or the identity of the self.

In this respect—but not only in this respect—all varieties of existentialism, both past and contemporary, are literary types of philosophy. The "existence" they talk about is human existence as directly and immediately experienced by the individual himself, not the objective structure of his life as it appears to an outside observer, whether scientist or historian. Time—or any other existentialist category—is meaningful only within the same context of personal experience, not within the context of nature. It would be ridiculous to say that Bergson's or Heidegger's theories, whatever we wish to think of them, make a contribution to the solution of time in quantum mechanics; and no one, so far as I know, has ever made such a claim. It is a different question whether they make a contribution to clarifying the "significance" of time as we experience it in our own personal lives and as we relate it to the biography and identity of the self. From this point of view, literature, too, has always been "existential"; for it has dealt only with those aspects of time believed to be significant in the lives of human beings. It is no accident, therefore, that existentialist writers have been predominantly *hommes de lettres* rather than experts in some scientific discipline; that an analysis of art and literature is invariably a central and integral part of their philosophies rather than a tangential, peripheral aspect as it is in most scientific philosophies; and that their methodology is analogous to that of literature in that they appeal to the world of inner experience, subjective states of mind, and the total configuration of a man's life rather than to objective criteria of evidence and proof acknowledged by a scientific method. This correspondence between literature and what I have called literary types of philosophy is worked out in the last chapter.

Time as experienced, therefore, is an indispensable category for life. In applying this category to a description of human life, however, whether literary or scientific, we are again confronted by a peculiar dilemma. On the one hand, time is of the essence; on the other hand, the nature of time and the experiences in time are such that they seem to defeat the object of this description: the possibility of reconstructing and justifying the notion of a continuous life or identical self. And it does not make any difference whether we look upon time as a part of nature or as a part of our personal experience. The *qualitative* aspects of time in experiences and the *quantitative* units of physical time seem to give rise to the same dilemma: both seem to be discontinuous, different, and unrelated; hence, incompatible with the common belief that the life of a person exhibits some sense of continuity, relatedness, and identity. The problem here is particularly acute because it emerges within the context of experience.[18]

Literature has often played with variations on this dilemma. Perhaps Heraclitus was the first to worry explicitly about how we can step into the *same* river twice, since new—i.e., *different*—waters are constantly rushing by. The same puzzle obviously applies to the river of time within ourselves; again, it is difficult to see how we can dip into the same river of our own selves, whether past or present, if the moments we catch are always different. What we are, we are only in and through time; but we are also constantly changed in and by time. Time makes us and unmakes us, both in the physical sense of the changing cell structure of the body—completely renewed, it is said, every few years—and in the psychological sense of a constantly changing stream of consciousness. What, then, is this self which is a function of the temporal succession of different events and their residues stored up in memory? What, if anything, justifies the common belief that there is such a thing as a person, self, or human life exhibiting some sense of continuity, identity, or structural unity in the midst of and throughout the kaleidoscopic changes characteristic of the physical body, momentary experience, and memory?

These are metaphysical questions of ancient standing and prestige which have engaged some of the best minds throughout man's intellectual history. I do not propose a new solution nor anything like a detailed analysis of these questions. I merely wish to bring out certain aspects of the problem of the self which seem to be directly related to some of the qualities of time in experience and to which the literary presentation of man seems to have made an interesting contribution.

The most familiar way of dealing with this problem, in the philosophical and religious tradition of the Western world, is to say that the "true" self, or soul, is a substance; that is, an entity separate and distinct from the changing body. Continuity, identity, unity, simplicity, and individuality may then be ascribed to this self, or soul, by virtue of its being a substance, since substances are believed to possess these characteristics. This is an ancient view in the intellectual history of man, which still enjoys, in spite of frequent criticisms, practically a monopoly in the language and thinking of modern man. One reason for its popularity is that it entails the comforting belief that the soul (or at least an essential part of it) is indestructible—that is, immortal. This view encounters great difficulties because the logical and/or empirical arguments on its behalf are not very convincing. I shall not discuss these arguments nor the frequent criticism advanced against them.[19] It is interesting to observe how little this criticism, though cogent and powerful, has been able to influence our linguistic habits and the general climate of thought. According to both, the concept of the self as something solid and substantial remains a more or less self-evident, inarticulate major premise. Apparently the "significance" with which the concept is charged tends to prevail over any difficulties encountered in explicating its cognitive "meaning." I refrain from discussing this view partly because the problems it raises would lead too far beyond the scope of this essay, partly because contemporary literature does not employ the traditional concept of a substantial self—though, as we shall see, it has made a notable contribution to the problem of the functional unity of the self.

There is another familiar theory about the self which takes the opposite view. According to it, there is no such thing as the self, and the traditional concept of personal identity rests on a mistake. Such is the result of Hume's analysis of the problem in the *Treatise of Human Nature*, but this conclusion had already been reached long before by thinkers, especially Buddhist thinkers, in India. For the Indian thinkers—as for some of their exponents in contemporary literature—the denial of selfhood is derived partly from a denial of time, partly from an empirical analysis anticipating Hume's.[20] As time is evil and illusory, so is the self born and bred in time. All mystic literature describes time as an illusion and/or evil. Perfect reality is invariably envisaged as being beyond and outside time; hence, the ideal life can be achieved only through a liberation from time, craving, and personality. "The more you respect a personality," says Aldous Huxley's protagonist in *After Many a Summer Dies the Swan*, "the better its chance of discovering that all personality is a prison. Potential good is anything that helps you get out of prison. Actual good lies outside the prison, in timelessness, in the state of pure, disinterested consciousness." [21] In his *Perennial Philosophy*, Huxley cites a passage which makes the same point in much stronger language: "He [man] findeth evermore his knowing and feeling [of God] occupied and filled with a foul stinking lump of himself, the which must always be hated and despised and forsaken, if he shall be God's perfect disciple . . ." [22] Selfhood is thus reduced to the level of a "foul stinking lump"—an expression that is quite common in the religious literature of the West as applied to the physical self, but not to the spiritual self. According to this view the self is at best an illusion; at worst, a terrible evil, because the same attributes are ascribed to time.

But the status of the self may also be threatened by taking time at its face value. This is the premise of Hume's analysis and of Buddhist epistemology anticipating Hume. Both are explicitly predicated upon the fact of temporal succession and variation in experience; and it is interesting that the literary treatment of time proceeds from the same premise. It is precisely because experience for Hume consists of "perceptions which succeed each other with an inconceivable rapidity, and are in perpetual flux and movement" that the self is and can be "nothing but a bundle or collection of different perceptions" without any kind of substantial unity, identity, or structure. "The mind," he wrote in an analogy reminiscent of Shakespeare, "is a kind of theatre, where several perceptions successively make their appearance; pass, re-pass, glide away, and mingle in an infinite variety of postures and situations. There is properly no *simplicity* in it at one time, nor *identity* in different; whatever natural propensity we may have to imagine that simplicity and identity." Thus " 'tis evident [for Hume] that the identity, which we attribute to the human mind . . . *is not able to run the several different perceptions into one*, and make them lose their characters of distinction and difference, which are essential to them." [23]

Hume's analysis of personal identity presented the most serious challenge to modern thought, for it seemed completely grounded in the world of experience and posed the basic dilemma in striking terms. How can that which is composed of elements characterized by "distinction and difference" be viewed as having some sort of continuous, unitary structure such as is ascribed to a person or a complete human life? Hume, of course, was fully aware of our natural propensity to impute identity to objects and persons; and he tried to explain the origin and basis of this propensity. He concluded that the unique relations constituting memory structure were "the source of personal identity for human beings"; the primary relations which he believed gave rise to this unique structure called the self were "resemblance" and "causation" (or associations).[24] Lord Russell has worked out a similar theory in our own days.

No doubt memory enters as an integral part into the construction (or reconstruction) of the identity of a person as depicted in a literary portrait; but the literary portrait has, I believe, invariably gone beyond Hume's analysis of experience by exhibiting a sense of continuity and functional unity of the self in the midst of temporal succession and change. Two aspects of the self are particularly relevant to this literary treatment. First, the self seems to exhibit, over and above the succession of different impressions and ideas, a tendency toward dynamic and economical organization. It is not only a passive recorder, but an active participant; it interprets, organizes, and synthesizes what it receives; moreover, it does so from an "economic" point of view, i.e., from the perspective of the self as a whole; and it is these functions of economy and organization that are believed to be characteristic of selfhood. Secondly, the self is experienced as exhibiting a certain quality of continuity. Despite the rapid succession of different temporal moments, and despite the physical and organic changes of the body, the self is not simply a convenient label attached to a bundle or collection of these elements, but seems to be a kind of structure exhibiting continuity and unity of which the individual is directly aware in calling himself the same person throughout his lifetime. Both these aspects are experienced as characteristic of the self, and give rise to some sense of correlation and integration among the multiplicity of heterogeneous parts which we associate with personal identity. Both must somehow be accounted for. Both seem to be neglected, or disregarded, in Hume's analysis. And both have played an important part in the philosophical and psychological literature since Hume, and have come to play a central part in what is often called "ego psychology" in our own days.[25]

Literature has frequently addressed itself to these aspects of human nature. It has always depicted man as a center of active, dynamic forces capable, or incapable, of controlling, synthesizing, and organizing the heterogeneous elements of experience into a functional unity, structure, and identity called a person or character. In this respect, Hume's affirmation with regard to the "rest of mankind" (excluding only "metaphysicians") that "they are nothing but a bundle or collection of different perceptions," does not conform to the portrait of man as the experiences of poets and writers have rendered it. Although the picture of the self as a substantial entity is conspicuously absent in literary works, the model of functional unity is constantly displayed. Man is shown not only as a repository of perceptions and memories, but also and predominantly as a center of active, *self-regulative* functions. And it is these functions that serve to convey to the person himself and to the reader the fact that a certain bundle of *different* experiences exhibits the *quality* of structure and unity which enables us to say that they belong to the *same* person. Similarly, the awareness of continuity as an essential ingredient of selfhood is invariably part of the literary portrait. In this connection, the intimate, reciprocal relationship between time and the self becomes most manifest; for the awareness of continuity within the self is correlative with the aspect of continuity or duration in time.

The correlation between these aspects of time and the self arises in two contexts: (1) within the temporal flow of the specious present; (2) within the relations constituting the memory structure, or personal past, of an individual. In both contexts, our previous remarks about time may now be applied to the self.

I

How is the experience of temporal flow possible, Kant asked, if the events or moments in time, like the clock striking the hour, are thought of, as they are in the physical theory or in Hume's theory of experience, as separate, different, and discontinuous? He replied that we must assume some unifying, synthesizing condition of the self to be at work, in order to make this phenomenon of continuous flow or duration intelligible. Kant called this condition by the formidable name of the "transcendental unity of apperception"; but the terminology is quite negligible; for what Kant meant was that even the simplest temporal succession of events in experience presupposes certain synthesizing and organizing functions of the self. The self, from this point of view, is not only a passive recipient of stimuli, external or internal, but an active center controlling, modifying, organizing, and integrating these stimuli. Kant recognized various stages of "synthesis" even on the most primitive level of sense experience.[26] He was perhaps the most influential modern thinker in calling attention to both the dynamic, self-regulating functions and the sense of continuity as characteristics of a "transcendental," functional unity or identity of the self. In other words, time has the quality of duration because some functions of the self endure through time; or, conversely, we gain a primitive notion of an enduring, identical self in and through the experience of temporal duration. Kant expressly refused to identify this functional unity of the self with the traditional concept of a substantial self.

All subsequent formulations of the problem in the modern world employ a similar "transcendental" vocabulary and method as opposed to the vocabulary of empirical psychology developed by Hume. Both time and the self, according to Bergson, are characterized by the fact that they are "unities of interpenetration"; hence, there must be an intimate bond between these two unities. The Bergsonian phrase, however, simply reëchoes Leibniz' definition of the self as a "unity within multiplicity." Commenting upon Hume's statement that "when I enter most intimately into *myself* . . . I never can catch *myself* without a perception, and never can observe any thing but the perception," [27] Whitehead replied in our own days: how can Hume assume—or how does he know—that it is the same "I" which he is using in the first and in the second part of that sentence? The sentence seems to presuppose a sense of continuity and unity which it denies. Time and the self mutually condition one another by "integrating" the separate moments of experience into some sort of unity. "The mental 'now' is a unity because whatever its items they conjoin to one significant pattern, a serial 'now.' To think of time as unifying the experiences of the moment makes of time the integrator of the mind; but the unifying

by the mind of its experiences of the moment can no less
be taken as an integration. That unifying of the experience
of the moment is an aspect of the unity of the 'I.' " [28] Again
for Sherrington this unity of the mind, or I, is nothing other
than functional.

Literary works, I submit, have always acknowledged the
interdependence of the two unities of time and the self (or
the characters and actions depicted in and through time).
Ultimately, this is what constitutes the unity of the work of
art itself, so that there is a functional correlation in three
respects: time, self, and the work of art mutually and re-
ciprocally exhibit the same pattern of continuity, unity, and
identity. In modern literature this correlation is expressed by
using the same symbolism for time and the self.

It is the "stream of consciousness" which serves to clarify
or render intelligible both the element of duration in time
and the aspect of an enduring self. The technique is designed
to give some kind of visible, sensible impression of how it is
meaningful and intelligible to think of the self as a continuing unit despite the most perplexing and chaotic manifold
of immediate experience. The continuity of the "river" of
time thus corresponds to the continuity of the "stream" of
consciousness within the self. In other words, the same symbol, "riverrun," expresses the same unity of interpenetration
within time and the self.

More specifically, this aspect of the self is conveyed by
the effect of the associative technique, or the "logic of images," operating within the framework of the stream of consciousness. For what binds the chaotic pieces floating through
the daydreams and fantasies of an individual into some kind
of unity is that they make "sense"—sense defined in terms of
significant, associative images—only if they are referred to
or seen within the perspective of the *same* self. It is this "sym-

bolic reference" [29] within the same self which makes them significant. Otherwise, they would indeed be nonsense. They make sense precisely because the author has constructed the individual character in such a way that the apparently chaotic pieces are all interrelated by virtue of the underlying associations and because the reader is expected to reconstruct, at least to a certain extent, this network of significant relations. If this significance escapes him—or if the author fails in his construction—the work is "meaningless." It goes without saying that such a literary portrait, even if successful, does not establish any proof of the self as a substantial entity. It is rather a way of showing a functional or structural unity of the individual in the sense that the events depicted in or the associations aroused by the stream of consciousness would be meaningless unless we presuppose that they belong to the *same* person.

Moreover, in the literary context it is primarily the author who imposes this kind of unity and identity upon the character portrayed; hence, *he* represents the active, organizing, regulative functions of the self. The fictional character may fail (or be depicted to fail) in this process of self-integration. Thus it is commonly believed that the "stream-of-consciousness" technique in modern fiction shows the total disintegration of the traditional concept of selfhood. This is true in the obvious sense that the notion of the self as a solid, substantial entity has become quite untenable. Moreover, this method breaks up, separates, and analyzes contents of the conscious and unconscious life of man not previously treated so articulately; and the prevalence of this technique in modern literature reflects the increasing fragmentization of the self in the modern world. But the technique is also a subtle and ingenious way of conveying a sense of continuity and unity of the self *despite* the increasing fragmentization of

time and experience; for the scattered fragments of free association make "sense" only if we presuppose that they belong to the same person. In this respect, the literary portrait
outlines, within the aesthetic context, a concept of the self
which it is difficult to justify in any other language; and the
technique of free association may actually serve the function
of reconstructing, rather than destroying, a sense of personal
identity. Actually, the term "free association" is a misnomer
when applied to literature; for the so-called free associations
are always selected, controlled, and organized by the author
in order to achieve the effect of continuity and structure;
hence, it is he—or his work—that exhibits, even when his
characters fail to do so, the self-regulating functions characteristic of a sense of personal identity.

The correlation between these aspects of time and the self
within the specious present is particularly striking when we
consider again not a comparatively short stretch of physical
time, a momentary fantasy or daydream, but a much longer
unit such as a whole day or night. Thus it is a whole day
which constitutes the specious present in *Ulysses* and *Mrs.
Dalloway;* and the chaotic manifold of the temporal relations
in experience is explicitly contrasted, in both works, with the
relative simplicity of the objective metric and order of time
in nature. Joyce subtly injects, into the stream of consciousness, the hours as they roll by during the day in Dublin. Virginia Woolf achieves a striking contrapuntal effect by inter-
rupting the time flow of the various streams of consciousness
with the booming of Big Ben. These works create, as one
critic has said of *Ulysses*,[30] "the impression of simultaneity
for the life of a whole teeming city"; similarly, they convey
the impression of simultaneity for the teeming lives of the
individuals depicted. The "identity" of the city has the same
face as the "identity" of the persons in the city. The frag-

ments of lives in each are gathered together by a unitary, symbolic frame of reference, which also constitutes the unity of the narrative itself. "Action, character, and commentary," says Mr. Daiches in discussing *Mrs. Dalloway*, "are alike subordinated [to one theme]: the theme of time, death, and personality and the relations of these three to each other and to some ultimate which includes them all. Significance in events is increasingly judged in terms of these three factors." [31] Thus, ultimately, all three unities, time, self, and narrative, are a function of significant associations.

Finnegan's Wake is an attempt, on a vast scale, to render these unities within the prolonged present of one night. The book begins and ends in the middle of a sentence—a symbol for the cyclical theory of time which Joyce adopted from Vico, and also a way of showing how the beginning and end of the rivers of time and life form a unity within the most bewildering multiplicity. "In the beginning is my end . . . ; in my end is my beginning" (Eliot). Goethe expressed the same view in almost the same words: "Let beginning and end be fused into one . . ." [32] The "riverrun" of the Joycean world of dream and semisleep endures within the most complex and often obscure multiplicity. So do the individuals within the perplexing stream of consciousness (or unconsciousness) which includes elements from the waking life of the sleepers, their fantasies and memories, and from an almost impersonal world of history and mythology. [33] Again, these aspects of time and the self are strictly correlative; except that in *Finnegan's Wake* the symbolic frame of reference which provides a unitary structure almost fails to come off—partly because the significant relations are obscured by great difficulties of language and learning, partly because the specious present of the night is stretched to the limits of time and the self. The time invoked is the entire past of human history; and within this vast frame of reference, the personal identity of the individual characters may actually become suspended or transformed into an identity of human *types*. The continuity and unity envisaged in this long night, digging deeply into the well of human history, convey a sense of identity which is more "typical" than "personal." H. C. Earwicker is not only himself but also "Here Comes Everybody"; and the night of one H. C. E. and his family turns into a nightmare of the family of man. Thomas Mann adopts a similar frame of reference at the opening of his biblical tetralogy: "Deep is the well of the past. Should one not call it unfathomable?"—and the individual characters in *Joseph and His Brothers* reveal the same ambiguity between typical and personal identity as do those in *Finnegan's Wake*.

We shall consider later on the significance of this reconstruction of the self in terms of typical human situations or mythical prototypes; for such an undertaking draws upon memory and the dimension of the past that transcends the scope of the specious present. The transition, however, is perhaps not so unusual as is sometimes thought. Employing the same metaphors, Thomas Wolfe describes a similar experience.

My mind and memory *in sleep* blazed with a fiery *river* of unending images: the whole vast reservoirs of memory were exhumed and poured into the torrents of this fiery *flood*, a million things, once seen and long forgotten, were restored and blazed across my vision in this *stream* of light—and a million million things unseen, the faces, cities, streets, and landscapes yet unseen and long imagined—the unknown faces yet more real than these that I had known, the unheard voices more familiar than the voices I had heard forever, the unseen patterns, masses, shapes and landscapes *in their essence far more real than any actual or substantial fact* that I had ever known—all *streamed* across my fevered and unresting mind the *flood* of their unending pageantry—and suddenly I knew that it would never end.[34]

II

More important than the preoccupation with the momentary stream of consciousness is the functional interdependence of the two unities of time and the self with regard to the past. The quest for disclosing some sense of continuity, identity, and unity within the context of the personal past of the individual has engaged great literature everywhere. It is by no means confined to biographical or autobiographical documents such as Goethe's or Proust's remembrances of things past.

The key to this quest has been memory—its function in human experience, on the one hand, and its place within the objective succession and order of time, on the other. St. Augustine first recognized the nature of memory as a key to the structure of time and the self. He developed his *theory* of time after the earlier parts of the *Confessions* had shown, in *literary* form, how memory functions in the reconstruction of one's life.

Great is the power of memory, a fearful thing, O my God, a deep and boundless manifoldness; and this thing is the mind, and this am I myself. What am I then, O my God? What nature am I? A life various and manifold, and exceeding immense. Behold in the plains, and caves, and caverns of my memory, innumerable and innumerably full of innumerable kinds of things, either through images, as all bodies; or by actual presence, as the arts; or by certain notions or impressions, as the affections of the mind, which, *even when the mind doth not feel, the memory retaineth*, while yet whatsoever is in the memory is also in the mind—over all these do I run, I fly; I dive on this side and on that, as far as I can, and there is no end. So great is the force of memory, so great the force of life, even in the mortal life of man.[35]

All psychological theories since have emphasized the integral relationship between memory and the self. The past, as we have seen, differs from the future, among other things in that it leaves records, whereas the future does not. And the mind is a recording instrument of peculiar sensitivity and complexity: I know who I am by virtue of the records and relations constituting the memory which I call my own, and which differs from the memory structure of others.

The question may now be asked, how are the different patterns of my memory related to each other at different times? It is one thing to say that the principle of association accounts for a unified memory field at a given cross section of time; but how can we account, if at all, for the sense of continuity which the individual feels to exist between the different contents of his memory at different times; how can we explain the unique relationship each individual has (or believes he has) to the sum total of his past life? The point is to show, if possible, not only the associative network of relations constituting a unified field at a given time but also the quality of continuity prevailing among the different memory structures at different times; in short, how the mind can "run the different perceptions and memories into one." This Hume thought was impossible. And it is with respect to the solution of this problem that I think Proust made a memorable contribution.

Literary portraits in general have always shown that the principle of "unity within multiplicity" must be extended beyond the present to the entire past of an individual in order to exhibit the distinctive, characteristic pattern of responses and associations which we call his "character." Proust's *Remembrance of Things Past*, however, is a unique document for two reasons: first, because it reveals how the reconstruction of the self corresponds to the recapture of time in experience; second, because this quest for time and the self assigns to memory a unique function and employs a method for disclosing a sense of continuity between the different contents of one's memory. Memory becomes a symbol for the active, creative, regulative functions of the self. And this creative aspect of memory (in art) discloses a unified, coherent structure of the self, which cannot be otherwise recovered in experience.

Wolfe, whose indebtedness to Proust (as well as to Joyce) has often been noted,[36] set out on a similar task. There is an interesting passage in *The Story of a Novel* in which he describes, in strictly Proustian terms, the infinite complexity and intensity of his memories, as a clue to his being a writer: "My memory was at work night and day, in a way that I could at first neither check nor control and that swarmed unbidden in a stream of blazing pageantry across my mind, with the million forms and substances of the life that I had left, which was my own, America." Then follows the flow of free associations by which he discovers himself and America in Paris: the iron railing along the boardwalk at Atlantic City ("I could see it instantly just the way it was"); the bridge across the river; the sound of the trains, or a milk wagon as it entered an American street at the first gray of the morning ("most lonely and haunting of all the sounds I know"); the wooden shed out in the country; the bird song rising in the street; and all the multitude of sounds and sights and smells and tastes of city streets and houses, faces and people, which had lodged themselves in his memory. All this sounds just like Proust, even to the point of including "the faces, cities, streets, and landscapes yet unseen and long imagined" and singling out their *essence* as "far more real than any actual or substantial fact that I had ever known."

What is more important, however, is that Wolfe also realized that these apparently chaotic impressions and associations were the source of the creative activity within himself, and that the object of his life and work was "to *organize* the whole series [of impressions] into a harmonious and coherent *union*." The unified structure of his own life was to be exhibited in and through the continuity and unity of the work constructed out of the synthesis of memory and imagination.

I would sit there, looking out upon the Avenue de l'Opéra and my life would ache with the whole memory of it. . . . And when I understood this thing, I saw that I must find for myself the tongue to utter what I knew but could not say. And from the moment of that discovery, the line and purpose of my life was shaped. The end toward which every energy of my life and talent would be henceforth directed was in such a way as this defined. It was as if I had discovered a whole new universe of chemical elements and had begun to see certain *relations* between some of them but had by no means begun to *organize the whole series into a harmonious and coherent union*. From this time on, I think my efforts might be described as the effort to complete that organization, to discover that articulation for which I strove, to bring about that final coherent union.[37]

Whatever one may think of Wolfe's success in this enterprise,[38] there is no doubt that the method he chose to convey the notion of a continuing, coherent self in the structure of his work followed along the lines previously worked out by Proust. There is also no doubt that Proust worked out the interdependence of memory, the process of artistic creation, and the self much more explicitly and beautifully than Wolfe.

Proust's achievement is all the more remarkable because he accepted the premise that the individual, momentary impressions are separate, distinct, and discontinuous: they are "isolated, enclosed, immobile, arrested, and lost." Hence Proust concluded that even the continuity and unity ascribed to a single passion, like love or jealousy, may be an illusion: "What we believe to be our love, our jealousy is not one and the same passion, *continuous* and *indivisible*. It is composed of an infinity of successive loves, different jealousies which are ephemeral, but which, through their uninterrupted multitude give the impression of continuity, the illusion of unity." [39] If this be true of a single passion, it applies all the more so to the alleged unity, stability, and permanence of the self, or the belief that "our personality is built about a hard and changeless core, is a sort of spiritual statue." [40] Maurois quotes some interesting passages from Proust's unpublished letters and notes:

My life, as I saw it, presented me with the spectacle of a succession of periods, so occurring that, but for the brief space of time, nothing of that which had been the sustaining force of one continued to exist at all in that which followed it. I saw human life as a complex from which the support of an individual, identical, and permanent "self" was so conspicuously absent, was something so useless for the future, so far extended into the past, that death might just as well intervene at this point or that, because it could never mark a conclusion that was other than arbitrary. . . . The disintegration of the self is a continuous death . . . the natural stability which we assume to exist in others is as unreal as our own. [41]

These are empirical observations and conclusions in the spirit of Hume's refutations of personal identity. They anticipate the theme of the disintegration of the self, and its special significance in the face of death, which we shall find to be an important element in modern man's attitude toward time. Yet Proust also had "an intuition of himself as an absolute entity" [42] and embarked upon the task of rendering, in the nonlogical symbolism of art, a meaning of continuity and unity of time and the self which did not seem to be warranted on the basis of the empirical, skeptical premises. "One is no longer a person. How then, seeking one's mind, one's personality as one seeks for a thing that is lost, does one recover one's own self rather than any other?" [43] To begin with a full awareness that, on empirical and logical grounds, the self seems to be an elusive and illusory entity and to end up by finding, or rediscovering, a meaning of self-identity despite the original premise—this transition marks the fascinating dialectic in Proust's thought and work. It is accomplished by an employment of memory in the sense of creative imagination which differs radically from Hume's limited recognition of memory as a function of habit.

Like Bergson whom he followed in this as in other respects,[44] Proust distinguished two kinds of memory: a memory formed by habit and a memory consisting of unique events. The distinction was not so original as the function which Bergson and Proust assigned to the second type of memory. It was generally known that human beings not only remembered things by habit, that is, by a process of conditioning through frequent repetition, but also remembered events that happened only once, were never repeated, and could never be repeated. It was also known that the second type of memory could not be explained by association based upon frequent repetition. What was new in Bergson and Proust and others was that this type of memory—the recollection of single, unique, unrepeatable experiences—was assigned a special function in the quest for the recovery of time and the self.

The recollection of these single events in their original, qualitative content, the good-night kiss, the bell at the gate, the books in the library, the magic lantern, the hawthorn in bloom, the *madeleine*, the curbstone, the clatter of a fork or spoon—the recollection of these and a multitude of other events serves to convey a meaning of selfhood which could not be elicited from the contents of immediate experience. These recollections, together with their significant associations, set the process of creative imagination in operation and sustain it. Creative imagination is creative recall. Recollection is an activity, an operation[45]—not the passive reproduction of habitual memory responses. To construct a work of art is to re-construct the world of experience and the self. And thus a concept of the self emerges, through the act of creative recall translated into a process of artistic creation, displaying characteristics of unity and continuity which could not be attributed to the self as given in immediate experience. Experiences re-collected in tranquillity reveal a quality which is often lacking in the "collection" of data constituting the world of immediate experience. Hence, memories may well appear more "real," as some people have claimed, than the original experiences from which they are derived.

The self so re-created may be said to illustrate what Kant called the "synthesis in imagination"; except that this synthesis does not produce the unity of an object in nature, as it does for Kant,[46] but the unity of the subject himself; and the processes by which this unification is achieved do not involve the Kantian categories. At any rate, the "true self" that Proust recaptures from the chaotic manifold of different sense impressions and memories is the self which actively and creatively organizes the multiplicity into some kind of unity and structure. Through this act of creative imagination (memory) and organization the identity of the self is exhibited and demonstrated within the work, though all the elements composing it are characterized by "distinction and difference." For Proust these unique events lodged in memory eventually become metaphysical "essences"; but this aspect, which we shall discuss later, does not change the fact that they also serve as a key to the disclosure of some sense of functional unity within the self. For the most part—and for most people—they are "forgotten," lying dormant, buried in the unconscious; fortunately, they may also float back involuntarily or erupt violently into consciousness, to be seized upon by the *conscious*, creative imagination of the writer as a key to unfolding the unitary structure and continuing pattern of his life. This is exactly analogous to what Wolfe tried to describe in the passage cited above.

Next, the act of creative recall specifically shows the sense in which a quality of continuity may be attributed to the self. Continuity is exhibited by the fact that the different contents of one's memory at different times belong together. This sense of belongingness, in turn, is shown by the fact that the recollection of a single, unique event makes it possible to reconstruct one's entire lifetime. The recollection of the *madeleine* is the clue to the reconstruction of Proust's life, which means that the sum total of his life is *potentially* co-present (or simultaneous) with this single event. Of course, it is only the total work which shows the potential co-presence, or simultaneity, of all the elements with the self (as in *Ulysses* and *Mrs. Dalloway*); but that the work rests upon this potential simultaneity of all the heterogeneous elements contained therein shows the continuity and unity of the self depicted in the work.

Thus Proust could write: "A single minute released from the chronological order of time has re-created in us the human being similarly released." [47] In Eliot's words: "Only through time, time is conquered." [48] Or Proust could say: "All the memories following one after another were condensed into a single substance." [49] This is a reply, within an aesthetic context, to Hume's logical analysis (and Proust's original premise) according to which the identity, which we attribute to the human mind, "is not able to run the different perceptions into one." Proust believed, and rightly so, I think, that he had *shown* by his work how the different perceptions can be run and condensed into one—not into a "substantial self," as Proust's words might wrongly indicate, but into a "single substance" in the sense of the self as a unified structure to which continuity and identity may be legitimately attributed.

That this is Proust's actual meaning is perfectly clear, I think, from the final summing-up of the whole work in the last pages. Once more he returns to the melancholy memory of his childhood (the beginning of the many volumes he has just finished) when he was waiting for M. Swann to leave the house so that his mother could come upstairs to kiss him good night:

I heard the door open, the bell tinkle and the door shut again. Even at this moment, in the mansion of the Prince de Guermantes, I heard the sound of my parents' footsteps as they accompanied M. Swann and the reverberating, ferruginous, interminable, sharp, jangling tinkle of the little bell which announced to me that at last M. Swann had gone and Mamma was going to come upstairs—I heard these sounds again, the very identical sounds themselves, although situated so far back in the past. . . . When the bell tinkled, I was already in existence and, since that night, for me to have been able to hear the sound again, there must have been *no break of continuity*, not a moment of rest for me, no cessation of existence, of thought, of consciousness of myself, since this distant moment still clung to me and I could recapture it . . . merely by descending more deeply within myself. It was this conception of time as incarnate of past years . . . which I was now determined to bring out into such bold relief in my book.[50]

In this sense, the author at the conclusion of the many volumes can announce quite legitimately, though somewhat paradoxically, that he will now write the books which he has just completed; for the story he has just told is the life he has lived, and in telling it he has not only produced a work of art exhibiting continuity, unity, and identity, but has also reproduced his own self exhibiting the same characteristics. And in this sense, finally, he could legitimately rejoice at his achievement, "though the mere taste of a *madeleine* does not seem to contain *logical justification* for this joy," [51] not only, as Proust thought, because he was freed from the fear of death, but also because, as Goethe expressed it, "he is the happiest man who can see the connection between the end and the beginning of his life." [52]

The relationship between time and the self in these literary portraits is an attempt to preserve and justify the belief that the self is a continuing, functional unit to which identity may be attributed despite the overwhelming complexity of heterogeneous elements of which it is composed. I have dwelt on these aspects of the self to some extent because, as we shall see in a later chapter, the significance of these literary portraits is greatly increased in the modern world where continuity and identity of the self are severely impaired or disrupted. It will be seen that the significance of these literary reconstructions is the degree to which they help in exhibiting and restoring certain aspects of the self which are threatened and obscured by the impact of time upon the life of modern man.

Here I wish to append a few remarks showing that the correlation between the recapture of time and the identity of the self also holds in reverse. If there are severe breaks in the recollective, imaginative reconstruction of one's past, continuity and identity of the self are impaired likewise. This is a familiar aspect of psycho-pathological conditions which often leads to a complete breakdown of the self. Literary works sometimes depict a similar phenomenon, as may be shown by two illustrations, one from the ancient world, another from contemporary literature.

The story of Oedipus as retold by Sophocles may be interpreted in many ways. In this context, I wish to point out what may be quite a peripheral aspect, namely, that it may *also* be read as the tragedy of a man who is suddenly and brutally destroyed because the continuity of time in his life is irremediably disrupted. A terrible gap is opened up: on the one hand, there is his past as lived and remembered since the defeat of the sphinx, the liberation of Thebes, and the winning of throne and wife; on the other hand, there is the past of his childhood and youth, forgotten, repressed, or simply falsified, and subsequently brought to light. Oedipus, therefore, may be said to have no self-identity. He is "in fact," that is, in terms of his own experience, two different persons—though in terms of the objective "facts" of nature and history he is one and the same. We say that Oedipus didn't know who he was, which is correct in that he failed to experience his life under the aspect of temporal continuity, which alone can confer a sense of personal identity. In his case, of course, the literary treatment does not attribute the break in the continuity of his life to any fault of his own; on the contrary, Oedipus is perfectly innocent on this point. He does not know whence he came, or where and by whom he was raised; or rather, others are responsible for concealing from him his true origin, history, and identity. But regardless of how we may wish to interpret these literary devices, the tragedy of Oedipus may still be seen in the light—though, by no means, in this light only—of the fact that the break between his two "pasts" was so severe and the consequences of this split in his personality were so disastrous that it was impossible to mend the broken pieces of the self.

A similar situation in contemporary literature, on a much lower level of artistic achievement, is presented in *The Great Gatsby*. Gatsby is also engaged in a quest—a futile quest, it turns out—to recover himself, to find his "true self," through a recovery of the past. The crucial break in the continuity of his life, the transformation of James Gatz into Jay Gatsby, occurs when Gatsby loses Daisy, the woman he loves. It is this "bad break" which is made responsible for the false, corrupt, and deceitful existence he has since lived. Similarly, it is the recovery of that loss, Daisy's love, which is supposed to restore the continuity of his life, mend the broken pieces of the self, and reinstate the true, "Platonic conception of himself." [53] The narrator says to Gatsby, as Gatsby is about to meet Daisy again for the first time in five years:

"I wouldn't ask too much of her. . . . You can't repeat the past."
"Can't repeat the past? . . . Why, of course you can!"
He looked around him wildly, as if the past were lurking here in the shadow of his house, just out of reach of his hand.

. . . .

He talked a lot about the past, and I gathered that he wanted to recover something, some idea of himself perhaps, that had gone into loving Daisy. His life had been confused and disordered since then, but if he could once return to a certain starting place and go over it all slowly, he could find out what that thing was. . . .[54]

Gatsby (or Fitzgerald) never did find out. The recovery of his "true self" failed, even as it succeeded in the case of

Proust. The split between his earlier self (James Gatz) and his later self (Jay Gatsby) is too deep to be mended; the "incorruptible dream" of pure, absolute love is an illusion; and the method of remaking his life (reëstablishing his personal identity) by staking everything upon undoing the loss of this love is mechanical and contrived in comparison with Proust's magnificent reconstruction of his own life. But the theme of the quest itself—and the significance it has in the novel and for modern man—is exactly analogous to Proust's search for time lost as a means for regaining the continuity and identity of the self.

Eternity

We must now turn to a quality of time in experience for which there is no correlate in the objective time structure of nature. This is the aspect of eternity. "A single minute released from the chronological order of time has re-created in us the human being similarly released." What Proust meant was that the single event remembered in all its qualitative richness and concrete reality seems to be freed from the date it originally had in the chronological order of time; and that the same holds for the self imaginatively re-created through this act of recollection.

Eternity, therefore, means timelessness, not infinite time—a quality of experience which is beyond and outside physical time. We have encountered this quixotic aspect of time in several contexts:

1. The recollection of the single event takes place under the aspect of "eternity" in two ways: (a) The act of recollection itself is timeless in that it seems to have no date or temporal index attached to it. It is a permanent or timeless possibility. The recollection may burst into consciousness at

any time or place, which gives it the quality of being beyond time and place—though *after* it has happened we can fix the date within the sequence of physical time and say *when* it happened. Only the fact that it may happen at any time seems to put the recollection into a timeless dimension. (*b*) What is remembered, the content of the recollection, belongs in the same dimension. In memory the *quality* of an experience is preserved in its original state—at least for some people, if we are to believe the testimony of Proust, Wolfe, or Santayana—immune to the passing and ravages of physical time. The thing remembered seems to be independent of the date when it happened; it acquires the quality of an "eternal essence." These "essences" are not like Platonic ideas, of which the things in experience are feeble copies; on the contrary, the qualitative richness and uniqueness of each thing as experienced and remembered constitute its essence for Proust and Santayana. There is very little poetry which is not concerned with preserving the timeless nature of certain qualities in human experience. For Proust, as we have seen, the quest for these "eternal essences" became the focal point around which he organized his life and work; for Santayana, they are an integral part of a metaphysical system—whether justifiably so or not does not concern us here.

My point is simply to show how the aspect of eternity, for which there is no cognitively meaningful correlate within the context of nature, emerges from or attaches itself to certain phenomena in experience. This kind of eternity, of course, is still conditioned by the organic, physical nature of memory, which presumably is a temporal phenomenon. This way of looking upon certain qualities in experience does not imply or prove that they endure beyond the temporal limits of the human mind. Nothing is said (nor can be said, I think) about the meaning of eternity beyond the mortality of memory.

Yet this mortality does not affect the poetic significance of eternity. Recollecting single events, long dead and past in objective terms, with the intensity, flavor, depth, and variety of the original experience, simply shows that—whatever may happen to memory as a part of the human organism— the content of these experiences is not affected by the date they bear. They subsist, to use a technical term, in the substratum of memory, which gives them the temporal status of a permanent "now."

2. Similarly, the potential reconstruction of the self through memory manifests an aspect of timelessness. A continuing, unified pattern of life is conveyed through the literary portrait in that the manifold of different elements composing the self—memories, perceptions, and expectations, or past, present, and future—may become co-present. This, again, must be envisaged as a permanent, or timeless, possibility rather than as something which is an actuality in the lives of most people. But to the extent that this act of reconstructing the totality of a man's life is possible at *any* time, it is again not fixed by any date. Moreover, since the self is envisaged as a functional unit in which different elements are always potentially co-present or simultaneous with each other, it also has the status of a permanent "now," that is, it manifests a sense of being released from the chronological order of time, however deeply it—like every other organism—is embedded in the temporal structure of nature. That all the elements comprising the self are potentially copresent at any time thus suggests a way of looking upon the self as "situated *outside the scope* of time." This sense of eternity does not entail or prove the fact of a physical or spiritual immortality of the self—even though Proust sometimes talks as if it does.

3. Insofar as it embodies the timeless essences recollected

in tranquillity or the timeless self recovered from the passage of time, the work of art, too, shares the same quality. It is timeless in disclosing these senses of timelessness, or in being a permanent possibility for such a disclosure. This has been commonly recognized; it merely states what a work of art exhibits: that "a thing of beauty is a joy for ever," that "it will never pass into nothingness"; that it is "an endless fountain of immortal drink." "Nor do we feel these essences for one short hour . . ." Keats, unlike literary philosophers, did not reflect upon the metaphysical status of "essences," "nothingness," and "forever"; but what the familiar passage conveys is characteristic of a long aesthetic tradition. The work of art captures essences in experience and is a permanent, timeless source for the recapture of these essences.[55] Thus the art object may be said to endure without a date, as the qualities incorporated in it endure, and the selves reconstructed through and in the work of art have a timeless quality.

These different aspects of eternity have a legitimate empirical basis. They are grounded in the fact that nothing in human experience is ever forgotten; no voice, trace, or engram wholly lost. Memory is indestructible, except for pathological conditions. If this was not previously recognized, as it was by St. Augustine, it was perfectly clear to Proust and many other writers in the modern world. What appears forgotten and lost is only pushed aside, buried, or repressed, i.e., not accessible to our conscious selves; the creative as against the mechanical act of recollection for Proust consists precisely in descending "like a diver" to the deep "strata" of the "unconscious self"[56] and bringing to light those traces, impressions, and associations which seem to have been lost. Thus we see again that these aspects of eternity are conditioned by the empirical, organic nature of memory.

Literature makes little sense unless we assume the per-

sistence of unconscious processes in human motivation—
however recalcitrant such an assumption may be to logical
analysis. It is interesting to note that the literary discovery
of timeless elements buried in the unconscious strata of the
self is remarkably similar to Freud's description of the temporal characteristics of unconscious processes in the mind.
"The events of the unconscious system are timeless, that is,
they are not ordered in time, are not changed by the passage
of time, have no relation whatever to time. Temporal relations, too, are connected with the working of the conscious
system." [57] Freud repeated the same view in a much later
publication:

> In the Id there is nothing corresponding to the idea of time,
> and (a thing which is very remarkable and awaits adequate at-
> tention in philosophic thought) no alteration of mental processes
> by the passage of time. Conative impulses which have never
> got beyond the Id, and even impressions which have been pushed
> down into the Id by repression, are virtually immortal and are
> preserved for whole decades as though they had only recently
> occurred. . . . It is constantly being borne in upon me that we
> have made far too little use in our theory of the indubitable fact
> that the repressed remains unaltered by the passage of time. This
> seems to offer us the possibility of an approach to some really
> profound truths.[58]

This timeless dimension of the Id recalls the closing lines
of Nietzsche's famous "Nightsong": "Doch alle Lust will
Ewigkeit,—will tiefe, tiefe Ewigkeit!" Freud's remarks, however, have not found too much favor even in psychoanalytic
circles; but I do not wish to deal with the technical problems
they raise.[59] I have cited these passages only in order to comment briefly upon their connection with the previous discussion. (a) They state in descriptive language what literary
portraits have tried to convey through poetic language or

through the construction of individual characters in the work of art. (b) They obviously do not permit any inference as to an objective meaning of eternity (or immortality) beyond this life or, more specifically, beyond the function of an organic memory. To draw such an inference would make nonsense out of what Freud had in mind. (c) This correspondence between literary and psychoanalytic statements on the significance of timeless elements in the unconscious suggests a more far-reaching analogy.

The reconstruction of the personality in psychoanalytic therapy resembles, in certain respects, the aesthetic reconstruction of the self which we considered in the previous section. Perhaps this is one reason that so much of the serious scientific literature in this field reads like literary fiction, and some fiction like a "case history"; or that one might speculate, as Goethe did, that a life well lived exhibits certain qualities resembling those of a work of art well executed. The psychoanalytic quest for the buried treasures and agonies of the unconscious also serves the purpose of reinstating a sense of continuity, functional unity, and identity within the self, which was impaired or lost. The "success" of such a reconstruction is partly indicated by the degree to which an individual comes to recognize and affirm such continuity within the stream of conscious and unconscious elements constituting his biography so that they are legitimately *his own* and not estranged from himself, and so that they give rise to a genuine, rather than a borrowed, sense of personal identity. And the "success" is also predicated upon certain active, self-regulative mechanisms of the ego through which this process of reorganization or reintegration is to be accomplished. Conversely, a great deal of psychoanalytic literature is concerned with the many causes and manifestations of the failure to achieve some sort of unification ("integration," according to current terminology) of the self because of radical breaks (repressed elements) in the temporal growth of the individual. From this point of view, a trauma would be a "shock" experience creating a temporal gap. The severity and succession of traumatic experiences would threaten to disrupt the "normal" continuity and structure of the self; for being repressed (or forgotten) these experiences are lost to the conscious history and identity of the person, though they still shape his character and destiny. Removal of them would be a kind of restoration of unity between conscious and unconscious processes, reassembling apparently unrelated and estranged pieces of the self by establishing a sense of temporal continuity between them.

We must now consider another aspect of this preoccupation with a timeless dimension in experience which we have also encountered before; that is, its affinity with mysticism. The emphasis upon eternity, in contradistinction to temporality, is an element common to all forms of mysticism, East and West, past and present. Mystic literature invariably affirms the existence of an eternal order of Reality disclosed in and confirmed by the mystic experience. "Looked at from outside itself, the mystic moment is a moment in time. But looked at from within itself, it is the whole of eternity." [60] Mystics in all cultures and all ages have always distinguished between an eternal order of Reality and the temporal order of nature and experience.

In making this distinction, mysticism departs from the analysis of time in both experience and nature. It translates the aspect of eternity believed to be characteristic of certain qualities within experience into a metaphysical, ontological category. Or, the aspect of eternity found in experience is interpreted as a warrant for the belief that there is an eternal order of Reality—though few statements can be made about this kind of Reality other than that it is eternal. Mysticism thus provides an example of how certain characteristics which are disclosed in the most personal, intimate, and subjective experience are externalized and objectified so that they are taken as evidence for the existence of a world different and more "real" than both the world of ordinary sense experience and the world of scientific knowledge. The metaphysical problem of mysticism is to show in what sense, if any, such an externalization is warranted. We cannot pursue this problem here, because this is not an essay on the nature of mysticism. I mention the problem only in order to indicate briefly in what sense mysticism belongs to, and departs from, our previous discussion of time in experience.

The metaphysics of mysticism also involves a peculiar revision of the term "experience." Experience itself is twofold: ordinary sense experience and the mystical experience. The former includes all the experiences commonly recognized, impressions, emotions, and ideas, whether observed from the outside or introspectively; the mystical experience, on the other hand, consists of only a few special characteristics, such as a sense of eternity, a feeling of union with the Godhead, a sense of liberation from suffering and the self, a state of bliss and beatitude, and a few other aspects which invariably recur in mystic literature—characteristics which are ultimately incommunicable, because words, too, are part of the temporal order of nature. Nevertheless, the content of this mystic experience always contains the reassurance that the natural order of things, including the self as experienced and remembered, is an illusion, deception, or an aspect of *Maya*.

Mysticism thus involves a denial of time both in experience and in nature. It does not distinguish one from the other, but declares both of them to be illusory and unreal from the point of view of the mystic experience which discloses a transcendent, eternal order of Reality. In place of our previous methodological distinction between time in experience and time in nature, we now have a metaphysical dualism between different orders of existence. This also explains why the mystic view excludes, as we have seen, the notion of personal identity. Since time as experienced belongs to the world of illusion, the self, too, reconstructed within experience, is but a delusion and deception. Mysticism rejects the concept of a self as a "foul stinking lump" belonging to an unreal world of time, and invariably pleads for a liberation from the prison of this self toward a *union* with some other kind of being, the Godhead, the One, or the Ineffable.

In these respects mysticism is a departure from our previous discussion of the elements of time in experience. It represents a transition from clarifying these elements within experience toward externalizing and objectifying them in a world beyond time, or it defines "experience" in a way that is altogether different from the ordinary meaning of the term.

From this point of view, too, Proust's "essences" are not mystical at all and provide no access to a mystical order of Reality, however much he may have thought so; for in the light of the true mystic vision, they would appear just as illusory, vain, and insignificant as the order of nature defined by science or the practical pursuits of man. This is a point not always noted in the discussion of Proust's alleged mysticism. To be sure, Proust wanted to be "liberated" from time in nature, "the chronological order of time"; but not from the elements or qualities of time which he recaptured in his own experience and imagination. On the contrary, these were the most "real" and significant aspects of his life. But it is exactly these experiences—the desires, hopes, disappointments, and remembrances of things past—which are rejected by the true mystic as futile, evil, and unreal. Moreover, Proust's vast work was dedicated to the quest of *finding* himself, his "true self," not to *losing* himself, as the mystic does, in union with anything outside the unity of his own life.

Thus Proust's essences, the self, and even the work of art he created would still be aspects of *Maya* according to an orthodox mysticism. What makes Proust a "mystic" in a different sense is that he referred to the qualities which he discovered within himself as if they had an external, objective metaphysical status. But this was—as it was for Santayana—in the tradition of a philosophical Platonism (rather than mysticism); not a Platonism in the strict sense according to which the qualities in the world of experience are feeble copies of the world of ideas which is composed of eternal, unchanging, indestructible forms and prototypes; but an inverted type of Platonism, because the qualities *in* experience had for Proust all the characteristics which Plato attributed to the ideas *beyond* experience. The dualism in Proust's world separates the timeless qualities in experience (and the self) from the changing objects in nature, whereas Plato distinguished both the qualities and objects in the world of "appearance" from the eternal forms dwelling in a place "beyond the heavens."

There is no doubt, I think, that this process of externalizing the most significant elements in experience as if they belonged to an objective order of reality was suggested to Proust as a way of coming to terms with the direction of time toward death. We shall return to this problem of timeless objects, and to aestheticism (or mysticism) as a way of gaining access to a timeless dimension, after we have considered the significance of the direction of time in human experience.

Direction and Death

The problem of defining the direction of time poses great difficulties for a physical theory. It would be altogether impossible to enter into the formidable, technical complexities of this subject. What we can do, and need to do, is again to give a brief sketch of the general line of thought pursued by an objective analysis of the direction of time, in order to have a background for viewing the entirely different approach to this problem from the perspective of human experience.

The concept of direction emerged previously in connection with the problem of order. It was then seen that an objective temporal order was defined by causal processes in nature, and that the causal order of events was exemplified by so-called irreversible processes such as unscrambling eggs. Now irreversibility, as Kant pointed out, is a criterion for direction as well as order; for to say that a process is irreversible means that it runs in one direction only, that is, from the "earlier" event to the "later," or from past to future. Time's arrow in nature, therefore, moves in the direction of irreversible processes.

Such irreversible processes are found in thermodynamics. In classical mechanics, the interaction of particles was considered reversible; accordingly, the description of these processes in the equations of classical mechanics was independent of the temporal index. It made no difference to the solution of these equations, or to the description of nature in terms of these equations, whether "t" was positive or negative, that is, whether time pointed in a forward or backward direction. From the point of view of classical mechanics time did not seem to have a direction.

This situation changed with the study of heat. Thermal, unlike mechanical, processes did have an irreversible direction, owing to the unavoidable loss of heat energy in a given system and the corresponding increase in thermal energy with regard to the universe as a whole. This phenomenon characteristic of heat processes in nature was incorporated in the Second Law of Thermodynamics and stated as an increase in what was called entropy. Now if this law is valid, it provides an opportunity for coördinating the meaning of the direction of time with certain objective, physical processes in nature. Time may be said to move in the direction described by the Second Law of Thermodynamics, or in the direction of an increase in entropy. If and when the universe should ever die of "heat death," or, to use less anthropomorphic language, if and when the universe should reach a state of perfect equilibrium without changes in energy states anywhere within the total system, time would stand still, that is, would cease to have a direction or any other topological property.

This view, as I said, raises extremely difficult problems, both empirical and logical, but for our purposes it suffices to note that any analysis of the direction of time in nature must begin with and center around thermodynamic processes,[61] in order to appreciate how far such an approach is removed and estranged from the direction of time emerging within the context of human experience. Whatever the scientific or logical status of the Second Law of Thermodynamics, there is a relation of irreversibility given as an immediate datum of experience and uniquely and unequivocally defining the direction of time in human life. This is the irreversibility of the movement of time toward death.

This theme recurs, from time immemorial, in the songs and thinking of man. "There is no remembrance," said Ecclesiastes, "of the wise more than of the fool forever. . . . Though a man be so strong that he come to fourscore years, yet his end is but labor and sorrow, so soon passeth it away and we are gone." Omar expressed the same theme more lightly: "One thing at least is certain and the rest is lies: the flower that once has blown forever dies"; and Herrick invoked the same image: "Old time is still a-flying, and that same flower that smiles today to-morrow will be dying." Mephistopheles (in Goethe's *Faust*) put it cynically: "For all things from the Void called forth deserve to be destroyed"; Wolfe poignantly: "The mystery of strange, million-visaged time that haunts us with the briefness of our days." However ingenious the variations, the theme is always the same: the direction of time in human experience is given to us, as a stubborn, irreducible fact, in the briefness of our days, the transitoriness of our existence.

This is, without doubt, the most significant aspect of time in human experience, because the prospect of death thus enters, as an integral and ineradicable part, into the life of man. There is no place for the significance of this aspect of time in a scientific theory except to say that it represents an accidental, emotional response on the part of human beings to impersonal, physical processes in nature. It is no wonder, then, that this explanation leaves something to be desired, or is thought to be inadequate; or that we can appreciate the objective theory only insofar as the phrase "heat death" enables us to relate it to some aspect of time in our own experience. It is no wonder, either, that this quality of time —the transitoriness of life, time's inexorable march toward death—should have become the vested interest of poets, religious writers, and nonscientific, literary philosophers.

Their frame of reference is invariably the progression of time in human life from birth to death. Existentialism, as we have seen, has raised this principle of temporality into a cornerstone for an elaborate metaphysical analysis of man. Insofar as man has any nature at all, it is that of being a time-haunted animal. The basic premise of Heidegger's analysis is that man alone among living creatures, as he grows conscious of himself, has a foreknowledge of his own death.[62] But this insight only restates, within a secular context, what has been a commonplace in a long religious tradition. What distinguishes Heidegger, and other nonreligious existentialist writers in our own days, from this tradition is not the problem they are dealing with, but (*a*) the conclusion that there is no escape from this inexorable human fate, and (*b*) that this conclusion is used as the basis for deriving all sorts of other categories believed to be characteristic of the human situation. These existentialist categories, for example, care, anxiety, freedom, choice, ambiguity, etc., are invariably placed in the context of the irreversible direction of time toward death and make sense only, if at all, when interpreted within this subjective context.

There are two different ways in which this quality of time may be experienced: a positive and a negative way.[63] "Time is invention, or it is nothing at all," said Bergson in expressing the positive aspect of the direction of time. The same thought is expressed in a recent statement by Mann: "What I believe, what I value most, is transitoriness. But is not transitoriness—the perishableness of life—something very sad? No! It is the very soul of existence. It imparts value, dignity, interest to life. Transitoriness creates *time*—and 'time is the essence.' Potentially, at least, time is the supreme, most useful gift. Time is related to—yes, identical with—everything creative and active, every progress toward a higher goal." [64]

Time, in other words, moves in the direction of "creative

evolution," or makes manifest the creative, productive element in the evolutionary progress. We speak of the "womb of time," or, in a curious mixture of metaphors, of "father time"; in short, of time as the begetter of all things, the permanent possibility of creation, novelty, and growth. Viewed from this perspective, time is a productive, creative element in experience—the permanent source of making and improving things, goods, and the self; in Aristotelian terminology, the permanent condition for converting becoming into being, potentiality into actuality, imperfection into perfection. The direction of time becomes the condition under which we cling to belief in the realization of hopes and aspirations, in the opportunity for creation and progress, in effort and striving as a means for personal happiness and salvation.

This is the positive way of looking upon transitoriness. The movement of time toward death is also the condition of birth and rebirth. Thus, from Heraclitus to Bergson, time is identical with "becoming." In the religious tradition of the West, this view is expressed by the belief that God performed the act of creation within time; in fact, created time along with and in the act of creating things in time.[65]

Such a positive orientation toward the direction of time in experience, however, is comparatively rare. It was not the orientation of thinkers in the East; and it was not part of the major currents of Greek thought. Both the popular mystery cults and the philosophical tradition set by Plato and Aristotle discouraged immersion in the time of this life in comparison with a timeless existence beyond this life. The *making* (or enjoyment) of things *in* time was strictly inferior to the *contemplation* of things *beyond* time. And Plato could envisage time in nature only as an imperfect copy of eternity beyond nature.[66] Religious tradition has always taken an ambivalent position on this point. Although God created the world in time—expressing thereby the most positive affirmation of the value of time as a medium of creation—religion has also, and perhaps more predominantly, emphasized the negative aspect of the direction of time: the fear of death, the vanity of human striving, and the hope of "salvation," not through the creative aspects of time in this life, but through membership in an eternal city of God beyond time. Even "The Second Coming" is always envisaged as an event suspending time in experience and nature.

That this positive orientation is so familiar in our culture—so that many people tend to take it for granted—is primarily the result of social changes during the last few centuries and the impact of these changes upon man's intellectual outlook, including his religious views. It is only since the "rise of capitalism" in the modern world that the religious outlook, more particularly the outlook of the Protestant-Calvinist sects, has come to affirm a strongly positive view of time in the life of man: Virtue is measured by efforts and accomplishments in this world, not by a state of mind, or by rewards in the world to come. The "good" man is the active man, the successful man, the man who has used his time to good purpose. Success and achievements during one's lifetime have come to be "signs" of divine grace and election.[67] Social changes set in motion by the amazing economic expansion have been so radical and revolutionary that this positive orientation toward the direction of time has become a dominant strain in the general intellectual outlook of the Western world. Time is the essence. Temporal progression is identified with human progress. And time calls for ceaseless striving, activity, and production. We shall return to this theme in the next chapter.

Goethe's *Faust* is a striking literary expression of this positive orientation toward time. Faust's wager is predicated upon the infinitely creative possibilities contained in the life span of the individual:

> When on an idler's bed I stretch myself in quiet,
> There let, at once, my record end! . . .
> When thus I hail the Moment flying:
> "Ah, still delay—thou art so fair!"
> Then bind me in thy bonds undying,
> My final ruin then declare.
> Es sei die Zeit für mich vorbei.[68]

The wager, from this point of view (and I am singling out this particular aspect), is a test of time. The test is whether time can ever have any other quality than that of being pregnant with or instrumental for new experiences, whether this quality inherent in the direction of time throughout one's life can ever be reversed or halted. It is a test Aristotle, one is inclined to think, would hardly have thought compatible with his idea of a "high-minded man"; yet it is precisely the kind of wager which modern man has generally accepted.

The human response to this test is ceaseless striving and activity. Both ceaseless striving and activity are ways of counteracting the negative implications of the inexorable and undeniable progression of time toward death. The ceaseless striving characteristic of the "Faustian man" (Spengler) is a way of forgetting time. The pursuit, or the pleasure of pursuit, has intrinsic value because it is oblivious of the goal pursued or the value of the goal; it is oblivious also of the ultimate goal set for every pursuit in life, namely, death. It enables the individual to live within the dimension of a permanent "now," without past or future. Thus it is not the "moment" which is rejected by the Faustian man; on the contrary, he lives in and for the moment. It is rather the idea that the moment might linger and endure which is unendurable. For if this were the case, ceaseless striving and pursuit for their own sake would stand refuted. From this point of view, Faust's salvation is perfectly consistent, even though the devil is cheated:

> The noble Spirit now is free,
> And saved from evil scheming:
> *Whoe'er strives unweariedly*
> *Is not beyond redeeming.*[69]

The theme of ceaseless striving is combined with the production of a work of great social utility, suggesting the economic component of this way of salvation. The progression of time is seen as the road of human progress. Thus it is not only the pleasures of the pursuit itself by means of which time may be ransomed. There may also be a "timeless" object redeeming the pursuit; for the things created in time may not only outlive us but endure beyond time, thus again partaking of the quality of timelessness and conveying a sense of immortality to mortal man. The moment of self-fulfillment, the moment of losing the wager, comes to Faust when he has the vision of the swamps drained and converted into the free home of a free people. This is the moment for which it is worth losing the wager, because the act of creation *in* time is seen as enduring *beyond* time:

> The traces cannot, of mine earthly being,
> In aeons perish,—they are there! [70]

This belief in ransoming time through ceaseless striving and/or through the making of a monument enduring forever is always counterbalanced by the negative perspective which Mephistopheles brings into the play. Introducing himself as "the spirit that denies; and justly so: for all things from the Void called forth deserve to be destroyed," he closes the death scene of Faust on the same note: "What good for us

this endlessly creating? What is created then annihilating?"
Again, this nihilistic orientation is based upon an explicit
denial of the worth of the past in human life and history:

> Past! a stupid word.
> If past, then why?
> Past and pure Naught, complete monotony! . . .
> "And now it's past!" Why read a page so twisted?
> 'Tis just the same as if it ne'er existed.[71]

This is the negative aspect of the direction of time toward
death: "Es ist so gut als waer' es nicht gewesen." It was
Goethe's genius to see that, even in the modern world of
ceaseless striving and unparalleled achievement, there was
still a constant, unresolved interplay of the positive and negative aspects inherent in the direction of time toward death.

It is the negative aspect, however, the theme of the vanity
of all human endeavor under the shadow of death, which has
been the most common response to this experience of time
in human life. "Vanity, vanity, all is vanity," sayeth the
Preacher. Things done in time are also undone by time. "In
a minute there is time for decisions and revisions which a
minute will reverse." [72] Or in a strikingly pithy phrase: "We
kill time; time buries us." [73] Baudelaire invoked the ancient
myth of Cronos devouring his own children. "Time devours
our lives, and the dark Enemy who knows us seems to fatten
on our heart's blood and grow the more." "Time swallows
me minute by minute as the deep snow engulfs a body frozen
stiff." "Time is a voracious gambler who wins at every
throw." "We are crushed every moment by the idea and
sensation of time." [74]

What is brought forth from the womb of time is swal-
lowed up again by this monstrous being. Instead of being the
creative begetter, time, or this quality inherent in the direction of time, now becomes destructive, evil, and hateful.

"And nothing 'gainst Time's scythe can make defense." Or: "And nothing stands but for his scythe to mow." [75] Thus the symbol of the man with the scythe, the cruel reaper, is added to Cronos, the devourer of his own children; and "wasteful Time debateth with Decay." "Ruin has taught me thus to ruminate." The inexorable progression of time toward death and destruction turns into the "tyranny of time"; "and all in war with Time," we try to throw off the frightful burden of this tyranny—*l'horrible fardeau du Temps*—only to meet suffering, anguish, and defeat along the way. For nothing can and does endure, according to this view, neither the works of nature nor the works of man, neither man himself nor his dreams and hopes. "Naught may endure but Mutability." [76]

It would be superfluous to give a detailed documentation for this negative response, which permeates not only our lives and literature today but the historical record of man's thinking and feeling at any age and culture. The pessimistic note of existentialist anguish and nihilistic despair is by no means characteristic only of the "decadent" literature of our times. Throughout history it has been a common theme of literature, both religious and secular. What is characteristic of our own age is that the negative response is hardly relieved by any positive orientation toward time. But the nihilism itself had already found inimitable expression in Macbeth's melancholy lament:

> To-morrow and to-morrow and to-morrow
> Creeps in this petty pace from day to day,
> To the last syllable of recorded time;
> And all our yesterdays have lighted fools
> The way to dusty death. Out, out brief candle!
> Life's but a walking shadow, a poor player
> That struts and frets his hour upon the stage,

> And then is heard no more; it is a tale
> Told by an idiot, full of sound and fury,
> Signifying nothing.[77]

Such a view carried to the bitter end is unbearable. Hence, "time must have a stop" for Henry Percy as well as Huxley. Time's flight toward death and nothingness must be reversed or halted. "Death, thou must die," is John Donne's cry, as it has been the faith of religious believers throughout the history of mankind.

To find a way of arresting or reversing this irreversible flow of time toward death thus becomes the most significant quest in the life of man—a quest for some basis in experience or human existence which is untouched by this aspect of time, which is beyond and outside time. We must therefore consider once more this quest for a timeless existence, in order to complete our previous discussion of time and eternity. For the significance of a timeless dimension in experience, the self, the work of art, or beyond experience can be fully appreciated only when it is placed within the context of the melancholy, gloomy reflections ensuing from the direction of time toward death and nothingness.

Religious literature is a rich repository of documents setting forth in colorful, ever repeated images, the futility of human existence in the face of death, and providing, at the same time, a way out of this depressing prospect by faith in resurrection, salvation, and life eternal. There is little that future generations have been able to add to what Ecclesiastes said about man's foreknowledge of death; but these sad reflections find a legitimate and presumably constructive place in the remainder of the sacred texts of the Western world. To the believer, this pessimistic attitude only tends to reinforce his faith and optimistic hope in a world to come, where time has had a stop and God guarantees life everlasting. This may not be the only reason for his faith in eternal life; but there is no doubt that this faith, or whatever grounds it may ultimately rest, serves to counteract the pessimistic conclusions drawn from the experience of time in this life. Whatever else religion may be, the denial of man's mortality has always been an essential ingredient of religious faith and has undoubtedly contributed to strengthening this faith.

Mysticism serves a similar function: The ultimate goal of the "Enlightened One" is to escape from the Karma of reincarnation, the endless cycle of birth and death, craving and evil, and to enter into a state of consciousness (Nirvana) which is timeless, hence, a liberation from the experience of time. Thus whereas Mann can write: "Potentially, at least, time is the supreme, most useful gift," Huxley, writing from the perspective of mysticism, can say exactly the opposite: "As for time, what is it . . . but the medium in which evil propagates itself, the element in which evil lives and outside of which it dies? Indeed, it's more than the element of evil, more than merely its medium. If you carry your analysis far enough, you'll find that time is evil." This is so, according to Huxley's protagonist in the novel, because "time and craving [i.e. the ceaseless striving of the Faustian man] are two aspects of the same thing. . . . Time is potential evil, and craving converts the potentiality into actual evil." [78] Although this is an extreme view, it is completely consistent with what mystic writers have always said about the worthlessness of time and striving. This is a striking illustration of how two diametrically opposed attitudes may be taken with regard to the direction of time in human life.

Aestheticism, such as Proust's, is another "way of life," [79] disclosing a view *sub specie aeternitatis* from which arises "joy" and "the highest possible peace of mind," in Spinoza's language. Art, as Proust was to say, following Schopenhauer

rather than Bergson, is a "formula eternally true, forever
fecund with an unknown joy, a mystic hope [that] something else existed . . . besides the void which I had found
in all my pleasures and even in love . . . , something from
beyond life, not sharing its vanity and nothingness." The
taste of the *madeleine* and all the other timeless essences en-
shrined in memory and re-created in art thus fulfill the function of liberating man from the anxious awareness of his own
death. "One comprehends readily how such a one can be
confident in his joy; even though the mere taste of a *madeleine* does not seem to contain logical justification for this joy,
it is easy to understand that the word 'death' should have no
meaning for him; situated outside the scope of time, what
could he fear from the future?" [80] In Eliot, the mystic and
the aesthetic components of this view are curiously blended:

> Time past and time future
> Allow but a little consciousness.
> To be conscious is not to be in time.
> But only in time can the moment in the rosegarden,
> The moment in the draughty church at smokefall
> Be remembered, involved with past and future.
> Only through time time is conquered.[81]

It is unlikely that Proust ever thought that the sense of
eternity he discovered disposed of the brute, stubborn fact
of physical death. He sometimes talks as if he did: "Perhaps
the resurrection of the soul after death is to be conceived
as a phenomenon of memory." [82] But there is independent
evidence showing quite clearly that Proust was not a believer
in immortality.

It is with great regret that I find myself here at odds with a
distinguished philosopher . . . M. Bergson claims that consciousness overflows the body and extends beyond it. Where memory
or philosophic thought is concerned, that is obviously true. But

such is not M. Bergson's meaning. According to him, the spiritual element, because it is not confined in the physical brain, can, and must, survive it. But the fact is that consciousness deteriorates as the result of any cerebral shock. Merely to faint is to annihilate it. How, then, is it possible to believe that the spirit survives the death of the body? [83]

What Proust meant, therefore, by saying that "the word 'death' should have no meaning for him" is to suggest that he thought art was a "way of life" placing us beyond the temporal perspective of death, eliminating—or at least helping us to come to terms with—the fear of death and the despair at nothingness which are so often an integral part of man's life if it is seen and lived only under the aspect of temporality. This may, of course, be called a form of "escapism," escape from life under the shadow of death; but it need not imply such an attitude. The phrase *sub specie aeterni* may, but need not, designate a withdrawal from life and reality; it may also describe more simply a particular way of orienting oneself within the world of human experience; a different outlook or perspective upon life; a certain detachment from the tyranny of time; an orientation around those qualities in experience which seem to reverse or halt the consciousness of time's progress toward death. In this sense it may be shared even by people who have no use for mysticism as an insight into a "deeper reality." [84] Such an attitude may then even be called a "way of life" or a "philosophy" (in the popular sense) as soon as the significance of this perspective becomes clear to the individual so that he will single out these timeless qualities, or the human art of preserving and recovering them, as the only aspects of experience *worth* cultivating. And he may subscribe to this way of life even though the majority of mankind have not felt and do not feel it worthwhile to do so.

These remarks are made for two reasons: In the first place, since the decline of religious faith, the aesthetic way of life has become one of the most significant secular responses both to the challenge of death and to the general pessimism pervading the intellectual climate of our age. The positive, secular outlook—the emphasis upon ceaseless striving and the production of useful goods as a way both of affirming the creative aspects of life and of suspending an awareness of death—is still an acknowledged trait in our culture and part of its official ideology. For a variety of reasons, however, as we shall see in the next chapter, this traditional orientation has lost a great deal of its former appeal. Aestheticism has gained by default, as it were, because of the decline or bankruptcy of previously accepted "ways of life."

In the second place, the appeal of aestheticism as a new way of life is not limited to the pursuit of Proustian essences. "I will tell you what I will do and what I will not do. I will not serve that in which I no longer believe, whether it call itself my home, my fatherland or my church: and I will try to express myself in some mode of life or art as freely as I can and as wholly as I can, using for my defence the only arms I allow myself to use, silence, exile and cunning." [85] In the end, it is the mythical Daedalus, the "old father" of infinite arts and crafts, who is invoked in justification and support of the aesthetic way of life upon which the young man embarks. For Joyce this decision was not the result of any mystical insight, but a reaction to home, fatherland, and church; and the aesthetics he subscribed to came from Aristotle and St. Thomas. Nevertheless, the reconstruction of his life, the forging of "the uncreated conscience of my race" through art, also became the only worthwhile, intrinsically valuable perspective within the stream of his consciousness and the history of man. And this positive affirmation of art was as much an "escape" or alienation from time and society as it was for Proust—even to the point of physical exile. But for Joyce it was mythology rather than mysticism which influenced his outlook upon time and aroused his interest in Vico's cyclical theory.

For there is yet another way of coming to terms with the pessimistic implications of the direction of time toward death which has also become particularly significant in our age. This is the cyclical theory of time, or the belief that there is nothing new under the sun. Nietzsche called it the principle of "the eternal return of the same." As old as Heraclitus, and as new as Nietzsche, Danilevski, Spengler, and Toynbee, the cyclical theory of time has had a long history and has found its way into various fields of contemporary thought—including literature. The theory is patterned after the cycle of birth, growth, decline, and death according to which we experience the direction of time in the organic world.[86] It is thus a theoretical projection into history, or the universe, of certain elements believed to be directly given in human experience; and its persuasiveness undoubtedly derives largely from this fact. The theory posits the changing cycle of births and deaths as the one unchanging, permanent, i.e., timeless, law of history. Again, I shall not discuss the status of this law as a scientific concept, but shall consider only its significance in terms of human experience.[87] It provides another way of envisaging a timeless dimension outside and beyond the historical march of time. It is a neutral response toward this historical, temporal world, neither a positive nor a negative attitude. The timeless law of the eternal return is indifferent to the value of the temporal manifestations of this law. Time may be, and will always be, a source of both good and evil. In fact, to accept this principle meant for Nietzsche to take a position "beyond good and evil." This value-neutrality, however, is usually felt by most people to contain a negative, pessimistic outlook simply because *good* (as well as evil) is ruled out by the eternal cycles.

In literature the cyclical theory of time is usually presented in conjunction with mythical themes. The world of myth has many roots and ramifications; and myths have fulfilled a great many widely different functions in the past. Our own age has witnessed a growing and continuing interest in mythology as a subject of study and artistic expression. Again, this renascence of mythology may signify very different things. In crypto-psychology and in political ideology, e.g., in the Nazi cult of the myth, it has been a powerful instrument for mobilizing and sanctifying irrational forces unleashed for destructive human ends. This must never be overlooked.

Yet the return to mythological themes in the great literature of our age serves, or is believed to serve, quite a different purpose: not to surrender to irrational, destructive forces but to domesticate them through the medium of art. The rediscovery of the world of myths by Joyce, Gide, Mann, Camus, and perhaps even by Lawrence, is meant to be a humanistic force; or at least a point of departure for exploring the possibilities of a new humanism, not for justifying, in the name of mythology, a revival of barbarism. Whether this is possible or not is a different question. But it is undeniable, I think, that the employment of myths in modern literature must be placed in this humanistic frame of reference. Myths are chosen as literary symbols for two purposes: to suggest, within a secular setting, a timeless perspective of looking upon the human situation; and to convey a sense of continuity and identification with mankind in general.

The myth is a "timeless schema," as Thomas Mann has said. It is timeless in that it is ever present, a constant reminder of the eternal return of the same. Thus Prometheus and Theseus, Odysseus and Telemachus, Orpheus and Euryd-

ice, Paris and Helen, Agamemnon and Clytemnestra, Orestes
and Electra, Oedipus and Jocasta, Abraham and Isaac, Jacob
and Rachel, Joseph and the wife of Potiphar, and Job and
his friends may be envisaged as ever present, timeless prototypes of human existence, as symbols suggesting the cyclic
repetition of the same or similar human situation. They may
be relived as signifying a situation enduring outside place
and time—even though they are expressed in the details of
an individual character at a definite place and time.

Thus it makes "sense"—aesthetic, mythical sense—for
Joyce, reviving the cyclical theory of Vico, to invoke the
image of the mythical Daedalus at the end of the *Portrait
of the Artist as a Young Man,* or to rediscover Odysseus of
Ithaca in Leopold Bloom of Dublin, or to tell the tale of
H. C. Earwicker ("Here Comes Everybody") as a parable
and myth of Everyman. Thus it makes sense to return, as
Gide did, to Oedipus and Theseus, to rediscover ourselves in
the mythical landscape, and to relive the same timeless con-
flicts and choices imposed upon us by *this* age and the time
of *our* lives. Descending deeply into the "well of the past,"
Mann recovers for us, like an archaeologist, the mythical
world of the fertile crescent. "The ultimate depths of the
human soul are also the primordial depth of time." [88] And the
same perspective is at work in the revival of mythical themes
by Giraudoux, Anouilh, Camus, Kafka, Cocteau, and other
contemporary writers. Thus Wolfe could "see begin in Crete
four thousand years ago the love that ended yesterday in
Texas," or be transported by his own love for Mrs. Jack to
Thrace and Macedon, or try to recover his own life—his
own "dream of time"—under the aspect of mythical prototypes like Cronos, Rhea, Prometheus, and Orestes. In Mann,
as in Joyce, the mythical figures often tend to lose their
personal identity, so deeply are they embedded in the cyclic

repetitions of the same human situation, so completely are they identified with previous incarnations of the same human type. This eternal return of situation and type is caught in the mythical symbol.

In this sense, time has a stop in the world of mythical images that reflect the cyclic patterns of permanent possibilities of human existence. But as a timeless schema the myth may also serve another function. It may be a symbol for a generic, typical form of human identity. The quest for mythical roots may not be a quest for personal identity but for an identification with mankind in general. Myths may convey a sense of temporal continuity and structural unity for the "self" of man. Perhaps this is what lends them a grandeur, a civilizing and comforting quality, despite the cruel, tragic, and irrational elements they contain and express. They may transport us beyond time and the exigencies of our own existence. By recognizing ourselves in the mythical images of past struggles, triumphs, and defeats of man, we may also come to reconcile ourselves to the inescapable limitations imposed, by nature and society, upon the human condition now and at all times. We may at least acknowledge our membership in the same human community, or share, within a secular context, in what religious language has called the brotherhood of man.

This humanistic message has been a major element in the rediscovery of mythical themes in modern literature; but it is characteristic of the employment of myths in art and literature of other periods as well. It is also, for example, an ingredient of Goethe's treatment of *Faust*, which we previously considered in a different context. At the end of Part I, it may be remembered, Faust suffers a collapse—caused by the guilt he feels for the death of Margaret. At the beginning of Part II, Ariel admonishes the attending spirits:

> The fierce convulsions of his heart compose;
> Remove the burning barbs of his remorses,
> And cleanse his being from the suffered woes! [89]

This is accomplished. When he awakens, Faust has forgotten (or repressed, as we might say today) what happened before and his responsibility for the crimes and the tragedy of the first part. In fact, the second part seems to have little, if anything, to do with what came before. Only in the end does Faust return, through divine intercession, to Margaret:

> My loved, my lover,
> His trials over
> In yonder world, returns to me in this! [90]

Thus after a long digression, the finale comes back to the beginning of Faust's life—just as the play as a whole brings together beginning and end through the prologue and epilogue in heaven. Seen from this particular perspective the strange second part may also be read as a continuation of the first, in the sense of bringing about a reconciliation with Faust's past, or of undoing the severe break which occurred at the end of Part I. Goethe, however, does not show this sense of continuity in very personal terms. Instead, Faust regains his "identity" by being placed in contact with certain general, typical situations of human life and with certain mythological figures (e.g., Helen or the "mothers") out of the past of human history. Faust thus acquires a sense of the continuity and unity of his own life through absorbing—or being identified with—these aspects of a generic, typical, or mythical heritage of mankind. Personal and typical identity are fused in a way which may also be found in Joyce, Mann, and other contemporary writers.

Perhaps this function of myths gives rise to the belief that they are profound symbols for a humanist faith. And perhaps even Aristotle, the philosopher of the pure intellect, had something like this in mind when he confessed at the end of his life that "the lonelier I am, the more of a recluse I become, the greater is my love for myths." To be a "lover of wisdom, i.e., a philosopher, is to be a lover of myth" (*philosophos philomythos*).[91] The humanistic message of myths acquires a special significance in our age in which the fragmentization and "meaninglessness" of time and the self have caused, as we shall see in the next chapter, increasing concern and disturbance. According to this kind of humanism, whether ancient or new, the community of man would presumably not be defined only in terms of an immortal soul, a universal reason, or an ideal and idealized image of man. It would be composed of the common irrational, or non-rational, aspects of human existence as well—the aesthetic images of which are reflected and "celebrated," as Thomas Mann would say, in the mythical tales and prototypes. It would be an aesthetic humanism, a variety of aestheticism as a way of life. There is no doubt, as we have said, that such an aesthetic humanism is meant to be constructive: to master, through the artistic re-creation of the myth, dangerous, irrational elements in man's heritage, not to exploit them for destructive ends. But the destructive alternative is always present, and poses a constant threat to an aesthetic humanism; for to evoke the timeless, mythical demons and to "celebrate" them is safe only if they are tamed and transmuted in the process of *genuine* artistic creation. The failure of aestheticism is the triumph of barbarism.

Chapter Three

TIME AND THE MODERN WORLD

THESE are some of the major themes emerging in the literary treatment of time. We have distinguished six aspects of time characteristic of literature: (1) subjective relativity, or unequal distribution; (2) continuous flow, or duration; (3) dynamic fusion, or interpenetration, of the causal order in experience and memory; (4) duration and the temporal structure of memory in relation to self-identity; (5) eternity; (6) transitoriness, or the temporal direction toward death. These aspects of time, I believe, are—explicitly or implicitly—characteristic of literature throughout the ages, including ancient myths and religious texts. It has been our thesis throughout that these themes have been common to literature because they are attempts to deal with qualities of time which are *significant* within the context of the experience and lives of human beings, though they are not *meaningful* within a framework of time as an objective property of nature.

Ancient as these themes are, and their variations, there is no doubt that they have found a particularly striking expression in modern literature; so much so, as we said earlier, that a contemporary critic could protest against the excessive time consciousness of modern man.[1] Our own discussion, too, was largely based upon evidence drawn from contemporary literary sources. Although it is difficult to make precise comparisons with earlier periods, I think Mr. Lewis' charge is true: time has come to play an increasingly dominant and overwhelming part in the lives of human beings in our age; and there are good reasons for this shift in emphasis. Thus the question arises: what are the causes for this increasing preoccupation with time in the modern world as reflected in modern literature?

Of Time and History

We have said that the experiential properties of time, neglected by science, are generally more significant for human beings than the concepts worked out by a scientific theory. This is true; but we are now asking the question of how to account for the *increasing* interest taken in these significant aspects of time in experience which seems to be characteristic of modern man and literature. Science, itself, undoubtedly contributed to this trend: the "fourth dimension" has become a popular slogan, whether or not its meaning is clear; and certain implications of the physical concepts of time, in contrast to its experiential qualities, have also caught popular imagination. This is reflected in the popularity enjoyed by science-fiction literature, which often plays with the logical possibilities of different time structures as applied to the ordinary world of man. But this is a comparatively minor point; the developments in the construction of a scientific theory of time have sharpened the conflict between time in nature and time in experience, but the conflict itself was felt long before these startling developments in modern physics.

Thus the original question still remains: how to explain the peculiar preoccupation of modern man and literature with these aspects of time in experience. This chapter discusses some of the causes contributing to the rise of time in the modern world.

One explanation often cited is, I think, inadequate. This is the view linking the theme of time and the temporal technique in modern literature with the importance of time in certain psychological theories such as psychoanalysis. The metaphor of the "stream of consciousness," with its technical corollaries of "free association," "interior monologue," and the "logic of images"—characteristic of a substantial body of contemporary literature—is obviously related to certain techniques and findings in psychoanalysis. We have considerable evidence of a direct influence by psychoanalysis upon the work of individual writers. Joyce, for example, himself the strongest influence in the elaboration and perfection of this literary technique, had direct contact with the headquarters of the International Psychoanalytic Movement in Zurich during the writing of *Ulysses*, at the time of the First World War, and was quite familiar, it seems, with the writings of Freud and other analysts. Thus there clearly existed a mutual influence; and the same is true for a number of other contemporary writers.

Although this influence is obvious and undeniable in the case of Joyce and others, an explanation of the function and predominance of time in the modern world and in modern literature in terms of this influence is inadequate for several reasons. In the first place, time is an "obsession" with modern man in general, and had reached this singular, central position in man's orientation in the modern world long before psychoanalysis arrived. Next, even as far as the writers are concerned, it may be said of them what Thomas Mann said of himself: "I did not come to psychoanalysis; it came to me." ² Freud himself, it must be remembered, always acknowledged a sense of priority for literature: "The poets and philosophers before me discovered the unconscious; what I discovered was the scientific method by which the unconscious can be studied." ³ Or: "The poets are valuable allies, and their testimony is to be rated highly; for they tend to know a great many things between heaven and earth not yet dreamt of in our academic knowledge. In the study of the mind, in particular, they are far ahead of us ordinary people, because they draw upon sources which have not yet been tapped by science." ⁴ Even Joyce traced the particular literary technique he perfected to a comparatively unknown French writer named Dujardin, who developed the method of the "interior dialogue" without indebtedness to any scientific theory.⁵ Furthermore, the method itself is not quite so novel as it is sometimes alleged to be; it was used by Jean Paul and was already perfected, to a high degree, by Sterne. What is characteristic, therefore, of the contemporary period is not that the experience of time as inner flux was suddenly discovered as a new literary insight but that it was more consciously and deliberately developed into a special technique than ever before. The deliberate choice of this technique was, of course, influenced by psychoanalysis—though "free association" in literature is never as "free" as it is in the therapeutic method.

Finally, and most importantly, the "interior monologue" must be seen within the context of other causes affecting the significance of time in the modern world. The predominance of this particular literary method itself must be explained. Although it is not an explanation, "free association" is a valuable clue: it suggests, and rightly so, that what I shall call the fragmentization of time and the self is at the core of the increasing preoccupation with time. Conversely, the quest for a reconstruction of the fragments of time in terms of a unified, significant pattern holds a central place in the thinking and feeling of man about himself and society.

This point will emerge more clearly as we consider some of the causes, partly intellectual and philosophical, partly social and cultural, which have contributed to the heightened and perhaps excessive consciousness of time in the modern world.

The general frame of reference is simple and familiar. What we call the modern world in the history of the West began with a series of radical, revolutionary social changes which gradually extended over the entire range of human actions, institutions, and beliefs. This was the period that witnessed revolutions in science and technology, political revolutions, religious reformations, an artistic and literary Renaissance, and the economic revolution called modern capitalism. There is no point in belaboring what is commonplace; I wish only to call attention to the effects these radical changes had upon the concept of time in human experience. The major effects, I think, were threefold.

(1.) There was a sharp decline or virtual collapse of the dimension of "eternity," which had been an integral part of the ancient and medieval picture of the world and man. Whether "eternity" was envisaged (*a*) within a religious framework of a City of God "unchangeable from all eternity" and holding the promise of "eternal life," [6] (*b*) within a philosophical framework of eternal verities and values, or (c) within a social framework of apparently permanent, fixed social and political structures (as in the feudal period)—all these attempts at postulating a dimension of eternity or a world beyond came to be questioned and obscured as a result of the new and wonderful dimensions opening up before mankind in *this* world and as part of the astonishing pattern of changes in human history. Time thus came to be experienced more and more as constant change and to be enclosed with the dimension of human life and history in this changing world. The concept of eternity was still retained within the religious outlook, but this outlook increasingly lost its force, function, and significance when placed within the context of the actual human and historical situation. It became a "belief" to which lip service was still paid, but to which there was little correspondence in terms of the reality of the human situation.

2. Concomitant with, but independent of, this decline of the dimension of eternity was the adoption of the quantitative metric of time in modern science: the familiar units of clocks and chronometers. This was an important factor contributing to the triumph of physics as an exact science, for it introduced precision of observation and measurement. Its success had repercussions in other fields.

a) The philosophical notions of clear and distinct ideas (Descartes) or of simple and separate impressions (Locke and Hume) may be looked upon as being constructed after the model of temporal units in physics. This does not mean that there was a direct influence but rather that the analysis of experience into sensations and impressions was analogous to the analysis of the temporal continuum into distinct, measurable units. As the seconds ticking off the chronometer constituted the simple measurable units of physical time, so the impressions and ideas succeeding each other constituted the simple, primitive data of human time. The criteria for both were alike: simplicity, separateness, difference, and distinction. Hume's theory is the most radical and classic expression of this model for an analysis of experience.

b) This intellectual trend was reinforced by what I shall call the social meaning of time, referring to the meaning which time acquired in the processes of production and consumption in the modern world. I shall discuss some of the implications of this social meaning of time in the next section and shall demonstrate that time as a unit of production exhibits the same characteristics as the units of physical time and the units of sensory experience.

c) With this breakdown of time and experience into simple and separate entities, a philosophical problem made its appearance which is characteristic of the early modern period and which anticipated, within the context of nature, the same problem that was later to arise in connection with the human self. What, if anything, held the separate seconds ticking off the world clock and the simple pieces and patches of sense data together? How was one to account for the appearance of, or the persistent belief in, a continuous unified structure in nature and experience, if the only empirical basis for this belief was the distinct, unbridgeable moments of time or the simple and separate sensory impressions? Why didn't the world disintegrate, or vanish, from moment to moment, as the self was in danger of disintegrating if there was no unifying bond between the bundle of successive impressions? The questions may sound rather silly to us, but their weight was felt by many thinkers during the seventeenth and eighteenth centuries; and it is worth repeating that the question (or quest) involves in either case, whether nature or the self, the problem of structure, continuity, and identity.

Several theories were put forth to meet this problem in the context of nature. Perhaps the most popular theory was the doctrine of continuous creation.[7] It was a medieval heritage, for it said that God provided continuity and structure—thus preventing disintegration and disappearance of the world and the self—by joining the separate parts of time and experience together in a continuous, invisible act of creation. God was invoked in a similar fashion, but more as a *deus ex machina*, by several other theories, in the seventeenth and eighteenth centuries, designed to take care of the same difficulty; e.g., deism, occasionalism, and the doctrine of a preëstablished harmony in the universe. All these theories, fantastic as some of them may appear now, were different ways of meeting what was then felt to be a real problem: to construct a realm of nature exhibiting order, uniformity, and continuity out of moments of experience, or primitive data, characterized by diversity, difference, and discontinuity. "Windowless monads" must call upon miraculous, divine intercession in order to see each other. God must pick up the pieces taken apart by man's tinkering with the machinery.

Again, the novel contribution advanced by Hume stands out by contrast with the views of his predecessors. He adopted the same empirical premise—simple, distinct quanta of experience; but he dispensed with God to join what man had rent asunder. (Even for Berkeley, God was still around in order to fill the embarrassing gaps in sensory experience when there was no one else in the quad.) Instead of God, Hume chose habit. Habit explains the causal connections, and therefore accounts for the apparent orderliness and structure of nature. The same causal connection which is established by habitual associations lodged in memory defines, as we have seen, the meaning of personal identity.

It is not easy to say what the correct interpretation is of

Hume's views about the self. It is possible (and perhaps likely) that he meant by personal identity the sense of functional continuity and unity which we have encountered in our discussion of the literary portrait of time and the self. For example, he compared the self not only to a succession of impressions and ideas making their momentary entrances and exits upon an imaginary stage, but also—in almost Platonic language and in the manner of other writers during the eighteenth century—to a "republic or commonwealth, in which the several members are united by reciprocal ties of government and subordination." [8] Such an analogy suggests that more than habitual relations is involved in the psychological structure of the self. In terms of our previous discussion, this formulation would seem to acknowledge that, in addition to the passive function of habit, the self also exhibits certain active, regulative, i.e., "governmental," functions, and that it is the latter (rather than the former) which "unite" the several members into a commonwealth.

For our purposes, it is not necessary to settle, even if we could, what the correct interpretation is of Hume's views on this matter. What makes his contribution so important is, first, that in the conceptual schema of impressions and ideas, the active, self-regulative functions of the mind do not find an adequate place; second, that the sense of continuity as characteristic of self-identity is disparaged or lost in the same schema—the mind "is not able to run the several different perceptions into one"; and finally, whatever the correct interpretation of Hume's views may be, there is no doubt about their influence. They contributed to, or have been understood—by his followers as well as by his opponents down to the present—as contributing to, a denial of a sense of continuity and unity within the self. They have become an intellectual symbol for the fragmentization, or disintegration, of the self as the only legitimate theoretical model constructed on empirical grounds. If the Humean view prevails as the only legitimate form of empiricism, it seems to follow that experience, or this interpretation of experience, fails to support not only the traditional view that the self is a simple *substance*, which it is not, but also—and more importantly—the view that the self may be *experienced* as a continuous, internally related and unified system of thoughts, feelings, and actions. Instead the self seems to fall apart into isolated, unrelated fragments of experience, just as the system of nature, at an earlier age, was believed to be constantly threatened by disappearance, if it consisted of nothing but a succession of distinct, discontinuous fragments of time.

It is for this reason that Hume's views have become so significant in the modern world—all the more so since this philosophical model of nature and the self was reinforced by the disintegration and fragmentization of time in history and society. We must now consider those aspects of time which are more directly concerned with the historical and social dimension.

3. With the fading of the belief in an eternal order, time came to be experienced more and more within the context, order, and direction of human history. Truth itself became a function of time, or the historical process, no longer a reflection of an "eternal" order of things. Again, this might be viewed in a positive way as a wonderful opportunity for constantly increasing the scope and accuracy of human knowledge (as in modern science), or in a negative way as always falling short of the "ideal" which exceeds and eludes man's feeble grasp. But whichever attitude prevailed, time was no longer the precious medium for the discovery of timeless truths. On the contrary, truth, especially about man's own being and evolution, was now a function of time in the

much more pejorative sense of being relative to the historical process itself. History became the only permanent, fixed substratum against which the varying manifestations of truths at different ages and in different cultures could be interpreted and evaluated.)

Thus the ground was laid for the different varieties of "historicism" which made their appearance in the modern world and reached their full maturity in the nineteenth century.[9] But before turning to these theories and their influence upon the status of time in the modern world, we may note some general implications of this shift. (*a*) Confined to the dimension of history, time pressed more heavily upon man than when human life and history were also viewed *sub specie aeterni*. Time, historical time, became the only medium in which human life unfolded and fulfilled itself. Its order was set by the causal relations constituting the history of man or nature, by the things done in and undone by time. It unfolded in one direction only, as a constant challenge or as a source of frustration, moving toward an open future of novelty and creation or toward a closed future of oblivion and death. Time became the great begetter and friend of man, or the great devourer and tyrant. (*b*) Common to both attitudes was the overwhelming realization, or rediscovery, that time confronted man with nothing but relentless change and transitoriness, that within the constant transformations of nature and society "naught may endure but Mutability." (*c*) Finally, the reconstruction of time in terms of history failed. History itself became a patchwork of pieces without a "meaningful," or significant, pattern either in terms of a theoretical model—an intellectual construction joining the fragments of time—or in terms of human values and aspirations.

This failure of historicism, which contributed to the fragmentization of time, must now be shown in some detail. But the combination of all three factors—the compression of time into the historical dimension; ceaseless, inexorable change as the only lesson of history; and the disintegration of any unifying intellectual construct in history—helped to strengthen the consciousness of time in modern man and literature.

Summary

Historical theories, analogous to the philosophical theories of nature mentioned above, attempted to impose a sense of structure and permanence upon the temporal flux in three ways.

First, history itself was raised to the status of a deity enthroned above and beyond the succession of temporal changes and the relative descriptions (or truths) elicited from the historical process. While the sets and players in the foreground of the historical scene were constantly shifting and changing, strutting and fretting their hour upon the stage, there remained in the background, permanent, fixed, and eternal, a mysterious substratum or thing-in-itself—the broad, majestic current of history in its totality; and it was this thing-in-itself which historicist theories attempted to grasp or adumbrate as the only lasting, permanent object (and truth) within the kaleidoscopic, chaotic changes of its temporal manifestations.

Secondly, the historicist theories discovered structure, continuity, and permanence by discovering a universal, or "eternal," law. Whether the historical law was stated in dialectical terms (as by Hegel, Marx, and Comte), in evolutionary terms (as by Darwin, Huxley, and Spencer), or in cyclical terms (as by Vico, Nietzsche, and Spengler), or whether the historical law was concerned only with "eternal" economic relations of supply and demand—the "unchanging" nature of the market of human wants—all these theories, despite their material differences, had one formal element in common: the so-called law was believed to be universally, or eternally, valid, and thus designed to guarantee a sense of order, continuity, and permanence within the chaos of historical facts.

Thirdly, these theories of history—except the cyclical theory—had another important element in common: they acknowledged, explicitly or implicitly, some notion of progress as a component of the historical law. The belief in progress permitted a teleological reading of the theoretical law in accordance with human aspirations; it reconciled theory and practice.

When historicism reached its climax in the last century, human history came to be explored and recorded on a scale and depth never attempted before. Moreover, all the sciences of man—biology, anthropology, psychology, even economics and politics—became "historical" sciences in the sense that they recognized and employed a historical, genetic, or evolutionary method. The "principle of temporality" [10] prevailed in all the human sciences. Social phenomena were recognized as "inherently historical." [11] The total effect of this development was to provide, on the intellectual, theoretical level, a reconstruction of the direction of time within the life of mankind (or before the origin of man) never encountered before in history. Moreover, it was an intellectual model, disclosing a coherent structure and an inherent rationality within the infinite chaos and succession of historical phenomena. History was the march of reason through the world of man from Pithecanthropus Erectus to Hegel. And it was inherently rational, not only as an object of science, but also as a moral agent. For the history of the world was also the world's court of justice.

Thus was born the notion of a "logic of history" unfolding itself inexorably and apparently beyond the reach of human wills and purposes. Sometimes this particular formulation seemed to envisage, or at least to suggest—as in the concept of a "classless society"—an eventual suspension of the dialectics of history, thus hinting at a dimension of "timelessness," i.e., a cessation of the dialectical march of time, even within the context of human history and society. These eschatological elements in Hegelian and Marxist theories—similar tendencies may be found in evolutionary theories—though obscure and perhaps insignificant in the total picture, are interesting reminders of the quest for a dimension *beyond* time, and for an escape from the tyranny of time, by philosophies which are completely grounded in temporal processes.

This is not to deny that these historical laws were meant to be descriptive empirical generalizations. The point here is that, in addition to this empirical function, they also served a function which could be interpreted as a secular substitute for a dimension of timelessness. Similarly, the descriptive historical law was invariably associated with the teleological concept of progress. In each case, this second function performed by these historical theories greatly contributed to their significance. A detailed criticism of them need not concern us here. We may simply note that the criticism affected both the descriptive and the teleological components of these theories. The descriptive law did not have the universal scope envisaged by the theories. And it proved equally difficult to extract a teleological meaning from this law. In other words, history could not be interpreted in terms of a *unified* theory constructed and organized around a universal law (as in classical physics); secondly, the historical model did not warrant the belief in a *unidirectional* progression of time toward a single goal.

This criticism is often put in the form of calling these theories "monistic," or "monocausal"—as against "pluralis-

tic," or "multicausal" theories of history[12]—but this formulation is not, I think, altogether appropriate. It makes nonsense
out of Hegel and Marx (or sets up straw men) to say that
they interpreted the sum total of history from the point of
view of one single causal factor, whether world reason or
economics. Engels explicitly insisted upon the multiplicity of
facts and causes determining the course of history.[13] What
these theories tried to suggest was something like this: either
they declared a single set of causes, say the economic conditions, as the *most important* causal factor; or they tried to
formulate a general law or principle in terms of these conditions around which the multiplicity of facts and causes could
be *organized* most effectively, i.e., objectively and predic-
tively—somewhat analogous to the way in which the principle of gravitation was the most effective way of organizing
the sum total of data in Newtonian physics, though the principle of gravitation did not, by any means, do away with
specific causal explanations in different branches of physics.
Marx drew this analogy with Newton's "laws of motion"
quite explicitly in the preface to the first volume of the *Capi-
tal*. This assumption that there was a general, rational, causal
principle in terms of which the multiplicity and irrationality
of historical facts could be organized, unified, and explained
so that history might at last become a legitimate science according to the model of physics—this ambitious belief and
pious hope broke down, together with the teleological im-
plication that this rational reconstruction of history pointed
the way toward a more glorious future.

The result was that the notions of a unified theory and of
a unidirectional teleology in history became more and more
untenable. This, in turn, had the consequence of undermin-
ing the belief that history had a "meaning" disclosed by such
a unified theory or single direction. The problem of the

"meaning of history" invariably contains an ingredient of what I have called "significance." It raises not only the question, what are the objective facts and the logical criteria for a *meaningful* description and *causal* explanation of these facts, but also the different question, how *significant* are these historical descriptions, the laws discovered, and the course chartered, in terms of human experience, hopes, aspirations, and values. The so-called monistic historical and evolutionary theories served the important function of providing both a sense of "meaning" and a sense of "significance." The historical law was not only believed to be empirically descriptive of the temporal progression of history; it was also believed to be significant, or value-charged, in the sense of justifying human belief in progress, a higher standard of living, a superior culture, a more perfect form of government, or a classless society. Thus a secular "meaning," or significance, was discovered in, or read into, the course of history which earlier philosophical and religious theories had discovered in the dimension of an eternal order of things, or in the super-historical direction of time toward the Second Coming of Christ and eternal salvation (or damnation).

The criticism of the basic assumptions of historicism—that there is a unified theory of history and that it discloses a unidirectional course—was a serious challenge to the belief in history as an advanced science and a source of value. The criticism did not impair the validity of historicism as a *methodological* tool for making objectively valid and meaningful descriptions; and many critics of historicism, such as Hayek and Popper, misunderstand this point completely.[14] There is no inquiry into the human sciences which does not avail itself of a historical, evolutionary, or genetic method. But the criticism did raise serious doubts as to the claim that history was an advanced science (like physics), which it is not, if it is a science at all; and it did impair the sense of significance extracted from these theories. Historicism as a method fails on both counts. Instead of a single law of universal generality, a methodological historicism recognizes numerous laws of limited application; instead of a single direction, it deals with multiple directions or no directions in history; instead of outlining a coherent, unified pattern of history in its totality, it is concerned with multiple, heterogeneous, and fragmentary "patterns of culture." It is in this sense that the contemporary theories of history and the human sciences may be called "pluralistic." They are pluralistic in that they no longer envisage and result in a unified theory. They generally do not recognize the quest for a "meaning of history" as a legitimate scientific problem, or else they come to the conclusion that history has no "meaning" or significance. Interestingly enough, this conclusion may be reached whether the problem is approached from a scientific, empirical point of view or from a nonscientific, existentialist premise.[15]

I shall leave open the question of how fruitful this approach is for the sciences of man. There is reason to believe that it is by no means the last word, as is evidenced by the somewhat frantic cry for an "integration" of the pluralistic multiplicity and heterogeneity of the universe of the human sciences. But here we shall consider these theoretical developments only insofar as they affect the status of time in the modern world. No doubt the universe of history as reconstructed by pluralistic theories has become both more complex and more fragmentary. History has achieved an enormous gain in range, scope, and detail, at the price of losing what might be called its density and consistency. It is like a vast empire which, having pushed its conquests to the farthest regions, is now in a state of disintegration, incapable of fitting and holding the pieces together under a unified command.

The world of history has become so complex and so fragmentary that the data no longer fit into a unified, significant pattern; in fact, they do not seem to disclose any rational clues whatever, but only a succession of changes so rapid, so unintelligible, and so uncontrollable that the individual feels lost and helpless—for it is *his* history which he does not understand and cannot control. Moreover, it is his history which no longer conveys a comforting, teleological message. Either it has no direction at all, or it has many directions none of which yield a sense of significance in terms of human aspirations and values. Given this "meaningless" direction, time is experienced as much more of a burden than it was when there were still theories telling us where we were going and that we were going upward. History may well suggest to man a "powerhouse" in which the past is "being ground to pieces [and] senselessly used up as so much raw material in the fabrication of an unthinkable future." [16] This senseless march of time understandably leads to flights beyond time.

Both the fragmentization and the "meaninglessness" of history were reinforced by the decline of the idea of progress, which had been a much more general and influential concept than any particular version of historicism of which it was a part. Progress refers to the belief that time is a cornucopia, that is, the most friendly, helpful instrument available to man in his perennial struggle for the good life or for the best of all possible worlds. Time is viewed as the supreme value, because whatever may be meant by "value"—and however much human beings may differ on this point—it can only come about in the course and as a result of time. It is difficult, if not impossible, for us to recapture the power and fascination which this faith exercised over men's minds during earlier centuries of the modern period, when a belief in the universality and perfectibility of human reason combined with the achievements of the economic, technological, and scientific revolutions to make it appear almost unshakable and self-evident. We have previously encountered numerous expressions of this faith in literary and philosophical works. Whether it was expressed in terms of progress, success, self-realization, or evolution, this belief obviously contributed to pushing the consciousness of time into the forefront of man's thoughts and actions.

It is much easier for us to appreciate the negative reaction to this faith in progress which, pricked by Voltaire's Mephistophelian ridicule of Leibniz' faith in the best of all possible worlds, and assaulted by various forms of pessimism in the nineteenth century (Schopenhauer, Tennyson, Hardy, etc.), has steadily declined ever since, until the prevailing intellectual attitude of our own age makes such a faith appear, at best, naïve; at worst, a dangerous illusion. At the very least, our present attitude is to regard the direction of time as value-neutral, as a medium for good as well as evil, and to doubt or reject any attempt to draw a positive moral conclusion from *any* description of historical and social trends. Again, we cannot review the large body of scientific and philosophical literature which criticizes and refutes the popular belief that the concept of moral or social progress is or may be justified in terms of our knowledge of historical and social processes. Usually the pessimism is much more pronounced than is indicated by this criticism of the concept of progress. Pessimism is not only the title of one of Spengler's essays but a general attitude or orientation pervading the twentieth century.[17] In Auden's neat phrase: "The situation of our time surrounds us like a baffling crime."[18] Time is baffling partly because of the complexity and fragmentization of events and people in time, partly because of the crimes committed in time, that is, the increasing awareness of man's intractable "evil" nature—as against the previous belief in his infinite perfectibility—and the mounting record of man's inhumanity to man.

Thus time has ceased to be a friendly medium in which human beings could still feel at home despite the collapse of the dimension of eternity. Instead, it is looked upon more and more as a medium neutral, indifferent, and hostile to man's works and values, a source of suffering and anxiety, and a reason for despair. It is not my purpose to evaluate the respective attitudes outlined here. There is no doubt that the belief in progress has sharply declined within our own generation, and no doubt that this decline has added another brick to the burden of time as it weighs upon human lives.

We can now see the significance of the cyclical theories of time, and their literary expression in the language of myth, in a different light. After the collapse of the religious dimension and after the failure of the "monistic" historical or evolutionary theories, it is not surprising that cyclical historicism, in one form or another, still exercises a considerable influence on the contemporary intellectual situation. All other attempts to deal with the increasing pressure of time upon the modern mind seem to be anti- or nonhistorical in the sense of rediscovering a dimension of eternity beyond time disclosed by religion and/or mysticism.[19] Cyclical theories, or mythical symbols, still serve to convey, as we have seen, a sense of continuity, unity, and identification with the history of mankind as a whole. If the cycles of the same human situation and type repeat themselves continually, "all time is eternally present." Moreover, cyclical theories avoid evaluations, or affirm the value-neutrality of time; they make, as it were, a virtue of this theoretical necessity. For, as Nietzsche proclaimed—and Spengler was to repeat after his master—man's greatness and hope for transcending himself and the historical situation in which he lives may be seen to lie precisely in his coming to terms with the inevitable cycle of birth and death, or the inexorable law of the eternal return of the same. Thus what is generally felt to be a pessimistic view may be given a redeeming interpretation. It may lend a sense of "distance," as Nietzsche said, a detachment and freedom from too serious an immersion in the affairs of the present, thus relieving us from the pressure and anxiety engendered by the "meaning-less" progression and repetition of events in time. It may provide a sense of continuity and unity between past, present, and future, both historical and personal, which would other-wise be lost. And although these functions may not be much in the way of comfort and a positive faith, they are appar-ently more than can be got from any other secular point of view.

Finally, the cyclical conception seems to be the only theo-retical frame of reference in terms of which a universal his-tory may still be written. This, I think, helps to explain the general interest shown in the works of Spengler and Toyn-bee, however much they may be criticized by the pro-fessional historian on objective grounds. The project upon which these two men set out has caught popular imagination: to attempt a universal, unified world history organized around a simple general principle or law—the principle of cycles in Spengler, and a mixture of the cyclical principle with the law of challenge and response in Toynbee. These works, therefore, are late, and perhaps last, attempts to make intelligible a sense of structure, coherence, and continuity of history in its totality. Thus, regardless of their objective validity, they undoubtedly serve to preserve or reinstate a sense of significance which human beings can derive from this vast, ambitious reconstruction of their past—even though they do not necessarily justify a belief in progress or a better world to come.[20]

The Social Meaning of Time

These intellectual trends, however, cannot be properly appreciated without a better understanding of some of the social factors influencing the status of time as experienced by modern man. The whole meaning of time itself changed radically as a result of social and technological factors; and this change, in turn, had far-reaching repercussions upon man's thinking about himself and his orientation in the modern world.

The idea of progress was not invented by philosophical theories, but rested, as we know, upon the solid practical experiences of the radical material changes which occurred in the modern world, first, as a result of the economic and scientific revolutions of the seventeenth and eighteenth centuries and, second, as a result of the even more radical changes initiated by the industrial and technological revolution during the last two centuries. Thus the "Faustian man" was primarily the expression of this totally new social significance of time in the modern world and only secondarily the reflection of a new intellectual outlook. Time was the essence, and of supreme value, because it produced things of value in terms of the market and the material conditions of life. Time was an indispensable instrument for the production of goods in an ever expanding market. Thus time itself came to be looked upon as a precious commodity, because it alone made possible the production of all other commodities. We still say: Time is money. It is equated with money because the commodities produced in time mean money.

This concept of time as a *commodity* has prevailed in the modern world. In contrast to the ancient and medieval outlook, time in the modern world has become more and more an instrument serving no other function than to produce goods for consumption and profit—hence the changed conception of *ransoming* time through ceaseless activity, production, and profit, in contrast to the Greek idea of ransoming time through contemplation of eternal verities and values, or the medieval conception of ransoming time through membership in the City of God and attainment of eternal salvation.

This new interpretation of time, as we know, has produced enormous changes in the social structure and has been the basis for that amazing expansion of human productivity in all fields of society of which we are justly proud as the achievement of the Western world. Here we shall consider only some of the effects which this new orientation has had on time in human experience.

The commodity status of time influenced its metric and value. The metric was calibrated after the temporal units in the productive process. Time was measured by the things done in time, by production figures according to the day, month, or year, by wages paid according to piecework or hourly rates, by loans and interest due at fixed intervals, by accounts opened and closed. In other words, the metric of time in the social processes corresponded to the quantitative, cumulative units of physical time. Actually, of course, the physical units were simply transferred to the social and industrial world, for the exploration and exploitation of social resources required adoption of the same precise, rational, and scientific techniques and devices which had made possible the effective exploration and exploitation of nature. But it is worth noting that, in this way, the concept of measuring time according to quantitative, separate, unrelated units, or fragments, came to dominate the social world as well as the world of nature. The structure of time in nature, history, and society thus differed sharply from the qualitative aspects which we distinguished in the previous chapter.

Moreover, the value of time became a function of the values produced and consumed in time. This caused a peculiar ambivalence in man's attitude toward time. On the one hand, time was money, the most precious value or commodity in the social world. Hence there was increasing anxiety about every fleeting moment and irrecoverable quantity of time, whether or not it was truly "additive" or "cumulative," whether the instrument was fully exploited or wasted. "Saving time" became a virtue like saving money. Time-saving devices became the symbol for industrial proficiency and progress. A "waste of time" was sinful—a negation of productivity and value, not a welcome opportunity for leisure and enjoyment. But there was another side to this coin. Time was useless as soon as it was worn out, as old clothes are useless; that is, the past was dead and useless; and "looking backwards" upon oneself and history was a waste of time. The value of time was directly proportional to productivity, inversely proportional to consumption: the more time produced, the greater its value; once it was consumed, it was worthless.

The fragments were useless when they were past.

> Past! A stupid word.
> If past, then why? . . .
> "And now it's past!" Why read a page so twisted?
> 'Tis just the same as if it ne'er existed.

Thus the temporal perspective in human lives shrank, because the past was essentially stupid and useless. Only scholars, cranks, and reactionaries were interested in preserving and cultivating it. Time as experienced by man came to exhaust itself more and more in the quantitative units measurable here and now. This inner distance from the past, its psychological eclipse, is again due to the cumulative effect of radical social changes. The past "is being ground to pieces" by the mill of inexorable, incomprehensible change. It is "meaningless" both as a theoretical entity and as a personal force. It is hard to understand the past; and it is hard to appreciate what it was like, because the present is so unlike the past. Former ages and previous generations seem strange and foreign; for their ways of life were radically different from our own. It is even increasingly difficult to identify with the changes in one's own personal history, which has been full of breaks, gaps, and displacements. It now requires a special effort, special skill and training, or a peculiar frame of mind, to keep in touch with the past, to reconstruct one's own personal biography according to a coherent, unified, and significant pattern. The *experiential* links between one's own past and present have often been disrupted as much as the *theoretical* connections in history.

Thus a situation has developed which is quite paradoxical in human terms: the barriers of the past have been pushed back as never before; our knowledge of the history of man and the universe has been enlarged on a scale and to a degree not dreamed of by previous generations. At the same time, the sense of identity and continuity with the past, whether our own or history's, has gradually and steadily declined. Previous generations *knew* much less about the past than we do, but perhaps *felt* a much greater sense of identity and continuity with it because of the fixity, stability, and relative permanence of their social structure. Despite the enormous knowledge we have accumulated about the past, the temporal perspective in the lives of individuals has become so fore-

shortened in our age as to condemn them to live in a perpetual present—not the experiential, qualitative co-presence
of all the elements constituting their own past recaptured by
memory, but the quantitative units of the present as defined
by the consumption of goods, news, and the instrumental use
of human beings themselves.

This foreshortening of the past is brought home to us strikingly by certain technological developments in the fields of
transportation and communication. That the world is tech-
nologically one is a commonplace to which we constantly
pay lip service. As far as the experience of time is concerned,
this means that it is a world in which all happenings are vir-
tually co-present or simultaneous. What happens now here,
happens now everywhere; while we are at one place, we are
potentially (with the negligible difference of a few hours)
anywhere in the world. But as the range of human experience
has expanded, its contents have contracted. Although any
experience anywhere is accessible to the human mind, its
impact is quickly exhausted and dissipated. It has become
more and more difficult to establish a relationship, or significant connection, between the fragments of experience by
which the individual is constantly bombarded and to which
he submits by adopting the modern cult of seeking experience, any experience, for its own sake. In terms of his own
life, the individual experiences the technological unity of the
world under the aspect of disunity and disorganization, as a
series of temporal flashes and successions dissipated and disintegrating within the moment.

The same trend is exhibited in the production and consumption of news. The historical record reproduced by the
daily "news" of our mass media of communication, though
vastly extended in spatial coverage, is temporally confined to
the immediate present. Communication of news rarely serves

to establish any "meaningful," or significant, relations between the events of one day and another, let alone one year and another; it rarely attempts to introduce any principle of organization, continuity, or structural relationship into the assemblage of isolated, cumulative facts considered newsworthy. News must be "hot," as we say, that is, of momentary appeal and significance, or it is not newsworthy. News must be "sensational," it must provide momentary excitement and titillation, or it does not sell. Again, what cannot be consumed now is worthless; and once it is consumed, it is worthless.[21]

This line of thought is another way of saying that technology has shortened time and expanded space. What I have tried to add to this familiar statement is the idea that technology has greatly foreshortened man's own perspective of time and, by enlarging his mastery over *physical space*, has also confined him increasingly to the *mental* and *emotional space* of the momentary present devoid of continuity and significant relations with past and future. Thus technology has expanded the dimension of physical space at the expense of time, but has contracted the dimension of mental "space" to the fragmentary moment of the present.

In terms of human lives, these developments have had personal repercussions, of which I wish to consider only two: the status of the family and the status of the individual, because these enter into the portrait of modern man in literary and philosophical works.

The position of the family in the modern world illustrates what I have called the foreshortening of the past. The decline of the family as a significant social unit in our world is due to a complex set of sociological and psychological causes. On the sociological side, it is primarily due to the conditions of urban, industrial life, with its special working conditions, economic insecurity, and social mobility and instability. On the psychological side, the individual himself contributed to the disruption of the traditional family pattern because his personal freedom could be achieved only at the price of a violent struggle against parental authority or an actual break with the authoritarian structure of the family. Both sociological and psychological factors influencing this development play an important part in the portrait of the family in modern literature. *Fathers and Sons, The Brothers Karamazov, The Way of All Flesh,* and *Sons and Lovers* are a few striking reminders of the general theme of the struggle between generations which is characteristic of modern literature.[22]

I am interested here only in the aspect of this problem which belongs to the subject of time. From this point of view, the decline of the family has contributed to a foreshortening of the past, or may itself be a reflection of this contraction of time in human lives. The past has shrunk, so far as it was preserved in the succession of generations forming a family and so far as the individual's identification with this past of his own family is concerned.

Modern literature has recorded several manifestations of this decline of the traditional family pattern. The individual may be depicted as asserting his own freedom and integrity only by denying membership in the family. This is the overt theme of the works cited above and summarized in Joyce's pledge: "I will not serve that in which I no longer believe, whether it call itself my home, my fatherland or my church." This protest is usually seen as an act of liberation, which it is; but it also entails a loss of temporal placement, continuity, and belongingness which was once achieved through membership in the family. The individual's life is confined to a much narrower span of time than when he consciously felt himself a link between several successive generations. He is increasingly isolated within the present moment.

Again, the individual may be depicted as emerging from an anonymous, impersonal social setting, apparently not belonging anywhere or related to anything or anybody in the world. He is a complete stranger, the literary version of the "displaced person," without a past and generally without a future. The most extreme portrait of this kind of individual, unrelated and undated, occurs in Kafka. The hero, characteristically, has neither name nor family; he is not only displaced socially, but also temporally, because the temporal setting is as negligible and nebulous as the social setting. The individual is often placed in a similar situation, without family and past, by other contemporary writers (e.g., Hemingway, Fitzgerald, or Camus).

Finally, the frequent, intense search for a recapture of the past, one's own, the family's, the nation's, or mankind's, which we have previously discussed at length, may now be seen as an attempt to recover oneself by discovering this sense of continuity with and belongingness to something that seems forever lost. This is what Proust is attempting in recording the decline and dissolution of the Guermantes way of life, or Mann in recording the same process of disintegration in the German bourgeois through the history of his own family in the *Buddenbrooks*, or Galsworthy in undertaking a similar task in the *Forsyte Saga*, or Faulkner in trying to reconstruct imaginatively the decline of a whole civilization in the South through the dissolution of the family and social structure. Both the quest and the failure reflect the same need for coming to terms with the loss of that continuity between past and future which was once provided by membership in the family. Both the quest and the failure are summed up in the title of Wolfe's final work: *You Can't Go Home Again.*

More important, perhaps, is the changed status of the individual; for it is he who is ultimately the focus for the changes in the meaning of time which are due to the ideological, social, and technological factors in the modern world. What he is, he is as a product of time; and time as he experiences it now reveals aspects which cannot but make him uneasy. It is from this point of view, I think, that we must look at certain views about the nature and value of man characteristic of modern thought.

Corresponding to the fragmentization of time, there is the view of man as an accumulation of distinct, separate atoms or experiences in time. The self is a bundle not only of impressions and ideas, as it was for Hume, but also of cumulative units of production, or—more accurately—units of productivity. The assertion that the self is composed of nothing but such units and does not exhibit a sense of personal identity or functional unity corresponds to the view that time is composed of the same kind of units. But if the self is thus broken up into fragmentary pieces of experience and production, it is a "divided and unhappy consciousness"; and the question of man's ultimate worth looms large and ominous.

For the social meaning of time deeply affects the status and value of the self. If the value of time is measured by what is produced and consumed, and if the individual's life is envisaged as nothing but an accumulation of these socially useful moments of time, the status of the self is obviously threatened. Instead of being endowed with intrinsic value, the self is of purely instrumental, technological value, just like any other commodity. Caught within the formidable pressures of time and the social world, the self is reduced to the status of what it can produce, accomplish, and achieve, or whatever other terms may be used to designate this purely instrumental relationship. Thus the notion arises—however subtly it may

be concealed for a while or under special circumstances—
that the individual is worth the price he can fetch in the
market place; not in the literal sense of the slave market,[23]
to be sure, but in the wider sense that human worth is predominantly a function of human productivity and success as
defined by the elaborate superstructure of the market place.

Thus time—being looked upon as a commodity like the
goods produced in time—ultimately converts man himself
into a commodity. To say that the moments of time are of
purely instrumental value, like the units of production, easily
leads to the notion that the accumulation (or bundle) of
such moments and fragments constituting the life history
of an individual also is of purely instrumental, and never of
intrinsic, value. Man himself becomes primarily a productive
unit along the assembly lines of society, or a commodity to
be used for further production.[24] He is worth what he is
worth here and now; and this value of the present moment
—and of himself as defined by the present moment—is determined largely by what he can do or has just done. His
price is set by what he "makes," as we say in a strangely
equivocal phrase; for the "making" may refer to his capacity
for production, for turning out the "stuff," whether it is
material, intellectual, or artistic; or it may refer to his worth
in terms of money, prestige, status, success, or some other
equivalent description denoting social achievement. The
general principle is the same: man's worth is invariably measured by what he has done or is capable of doing, rather than
by what he is.

This trend, of course, describes an "ideal type," in Max
Weber's sense of the term. It is exaggerated in that there are
perhaps few pure cases of this type and in that an older view
postulating the intrinsic worth and dignity of man still lingers
on in the official ideology of our age and in the actual prac-

tice of interpersonal relations. Nevertheless, the exaggeration has heuristic value. The writer in the modern world, for instance, is judged almost exclusively by what he has done "now," last month, or this year, by what his standing is on the current list of "best sellers"—the phrase indicating the commercial index which determines the value of the work and the man. If he does not produce regularly, that is, if he does not grind out a substantial quantity, regardless of quality, according to a "formula" (corresponding to the industrial "blueprint") which he discovered in his first successful work, he loses his public. The public loses interest because "interest" too, like the financial term, is an attitude which is measured in the same quantitative units. It rises and falls like the quotations on the stock market; its stimulus is usually spent within the immediate present; it is aroused and consumed within the moment. Interests are rarely sustained; they rarely endure; that is, they rarely have a quality of time in which the temporal moments succeeding each other, whether in the lifetime of an individual or in the reading of a book, appear as interrelated, continuous, organized, and unified. Thus the writer's worth—in terms of material success and self-esteem—depends upon whether he can hold the public's interest; and that in turn depends upon whether he can produce something that lives for the moment, though it be dead for eternity.

Such an orientation, it is evident, sets up a serious conflict with an ideological past which recognized and cultivated the idea of the intrinsic worth of the individual—as well as the derivative idea of the intrinsic value of certain works produced by man. Whether or not these ideas make sense need not concern us here. It is clear that the changes in the status of time have cut deeply and painfully into the status of the individual. What view can he legitimately entertain about himself? What intrinsic worth and dignity can he assign to himself? These are questions which might make a man feel uneasy and anxious, if he has to look back upon the moments of his life as nothing but an accumulation of worn-out pieces in a junk yard. Moreover, these questions demand an answer for other reasons. First, they challenge an ideological past that is retained even though it is strangely incongruous with social reality and theory. Secondly, they enter into most of the significant personal relations, such as love, marriage, and friendship, in which the individual is engaged with others. All these relations, and certain derivative concepts such as responsibility and loyalty, are predicated, rightly or wrongly, upon the assumption that human beings have intrinsic worth and that they are capable of entering into commitments which exhibit a sense of continuity, duration, and identity through time. None of these relations, or derivative concepts, can be reconciled with the view that human life consists of nothing but a succession of productive and instrumental units.

Not surprisingly, this problem becomes all the more acute the more man is likely to look back upon the accumulated moments of his life, that is, the more closely he approaches death. Looking back upon a lifetime, without the consolation of faith in an eternal life to come and without the comforting belief that this life has at least been a significant link in the over-all rational pattern of history pointing toward a better human world—looking back upon a lifetime spent as a succession of fragmented, isolated moments of experience and judged by the social standards of one's "time"—man may well envision death as the most ominous symbol of a "wasted life," a painful, bitter reminder of the lack of unity, purpose, continuity, satisfaction, significance, and worth of human existence; a betrayal of the "real" life the individual meant to live but did not live because he was a victim of "time and circumstances," as these are defined by the "realities" of the world in which he did live. Tolstoi's *The Death of Ivan Ilyitch* is the classic treatment of this theme in modern literature.

It is now clear that even the literary technique of the "stream of consciousness" or "free association" must be viewed within a wider social and ideological context. On the one hand, this method is itself a striking expression of the fragmentization of time in the consciousness of modern man; on the other hand, it is an attempt to overcome this fragmentization by showing that even this chaotic stream of time and experience contains certain qualities of duration, interpenetration, continuity, and unity in terms of which some concept of the self may be saved. The quest for these qualities, which we distinguished in experience and literature, is invariably motivated by the significance they are believed to have for human existence. And their significance has grown in the modern world to the extent to which these qualities, always irrelevant to the concept of time in nature, have also been neglected or lost in the social and human situation. The more the experiential structure of time is scattered into meaningless fragments of the present, the greater the threat to the status of the self composed of these fragments, and the more demanding the quest for ransoming those *qualities* of time in terms of which the human situation (or the individual life) might be reconstructed according to a coherent, intelligible, and significant pattern.

In this sense, the literary treatment of time may itself have human or philosophical significance. The existentialist movement in modern thought, for example, regards Tolstoi's story of Ivan Ilyitch as a philosophical document. This means that literature—a reminder of aspects of time and the self which may be neglected, buried, or lost because of our enslavement

to the physical and social categories of time and the self—
may bring to light, or may set us free to see, certain aspects
of human experience and existence from an entirely different
perspective. And although this conception of philosophy is
obviously a radical departure from what is meant by philosophy as a science, it is not, I believe, either intellectually
worthless or meaningless. It does, in fact, make an intellectual
contribution to what I shall call the *orientation* of man in the
world of experience.

Chapter Four

LITERATURE, SCIENCE, AND PHILOSOPHY

WE HAVE asked the questions: (1) what are some of the major elements of time in experience, as rendered by literary works, in comparison with and contrast to some of the characteristics of time in nature, as rendered by a scientfic theory; (2) what is the significance of this literary treatment of time; and (3) what are some of the conditions contributing to the consciousness of and the preoccupation with time in the modern world and literature? There remains another question: what is the point of this literary treatment; how valid are the statements made on behalf of the nature of time in human experience and expressed in literary language and symbolism: in short, what truth is there in literature; or, is literature a legitimate source of knowledge; and if so, how and why? These questions not only touch upon the vast subject of truth in the arts, but also lead to a consideration of the relationship between literature and philosophy.

Of Truth In Literature

Literature has always been prized highly, as both a source of pleasure and a source of knowledge. The pleasure we derive from a poetic work is immediate and indisputable. It may not always be clear, as in the case of tragedy, why literature is a constant source of delight; but it would be idle to question that it is.

The problem of knowledge is more complex and difficult. In one sense it seems perfectly obvious that literature conveys information and knowledge. We say, for example, that we learn a great many things from Shakespeare and Goethe, Tolstoi and Dostoevski, Balzac and Baudelaire. Similarly, the present study is predicated upon the assumption that something is to be learned from the literary treatment of time. In another sense, however, it has often seemed puzzling that literary works can be a source of knowledge—since they are the personal expressions of one man's view of life and reality, and since they convey this view through the medium of a single example or the construction of a unique character or situation. Sensible images, unique qualities, concrete situations form the substance of literary works, and from this derives much of the immediate pleasure conveyed by art. But a literary work reflects one man's view of the world; and how can this subjective point of view convey knowledge which will command general acceptance and agreement? This question may be approached by examining several ways in which this problem of knowledge arises in the context of literature.

There is, to begin, quite an ordinary sense of knowledge. Literary works contain descriptive elements as they might and do occur in other forms of discourse. They may, then, also be true or false, as these terms are used in an empirical, cognitive sense. This is, I think, the basis for Zola's doctrine of realistic naturalism: "The naturalistic novel is simply an inquiry into nature, beings, and things. . . . The work becomes a report, nothing more; it has but the merit of exact observation, or more or less profound penetration and analysis of the logical connection of facts . . ." Like an experimental scientist, "the novelist is but a recorder who is forbidden to judge and conclude." He "should equally keep to known facts, to scrupulous study, if he does not wish to stray among lying conclusions."[1] Taine and William Dean Howells held similar views about truth in literature.

No doubt literature contains a great many statements which confirm this naturalistic method. They may be descriptions of people, who they are, what they are, what they eat and wear, and what they do and how they do it. They may describe the inner world of human passions and thoughts, what people say, think, and feel; or they may describe facts of the outer world: a landscape, the weather, a village, institutions, types of work, ways of making a living, tools, voyages, and foreign lands. Or they may be more general. *The Magic Mountain* contains a great deal of descriptive medicine, as does *Arrowsmith*. *Moby Dick* may be read as a manual about seafaring and whale fishing, *Oliver Twist* as a source book for the conditions of poorhouses in England during the nineteenth century. These descriptive statements in literature are a rich source of general information and knowledge. They could, if necessary, be verified by objective tests and criteria of confirmation. They are, however, *not* what is usually meant by truth in literature; and Zola was mistaken in thinking that they are the only kinds of statements which literature employs, or that his own works confirmed his theory.

Again, literary works may develop general theories attributed to a fictional character or expressing the views of the author. *The Magic Mountain* overflows with theoretical discussions of this kind. The characters in Dostoevski constantly expound theories on the nature of man, God, grace, freedom, love, and authority. Shaw may hold forth on evolution and socialism. *War and Peace* expresses Tolstoi's views on history.[2] Proust presents theoretical reflections on the nature of time, memory, and the self. Again, theories of this kind are *not* what is usually meant by truth in literature. For if the theories are advanced as the author's own views of what he believes to be generally true, they are taken out of the context of the play or novel and may be accepted or rejected independently, i.e., on ordinary grounds of evidence and reasoning like any other theory advanced by people who are not writers and poets. On the other hand, if they function, as they usually do, primarily within the structure of the literary work itself, we are back at the original dilemma. Either they are descriptions of what people think, feel, hope, and fear, i.e., they are reports about ideas held at a certain age and by a certain class of people and so fall into the category of descriptive statements just mentioned; or they are expressions of what the character created by the author might or would think and feel because he is the kind of person he is depicted to be.

In this case, the old problem reappears. The meaning of truth undergoes a subtle, but radical, change. For it is now not a question of whether the ideas attributed to a person are true in a general or objective way, but whether they are subjectively "true to" the person as he is presented. Truth is ascribed to a single case or a unique human situation and is measured within the context of the literary work itself. We may say this is a "true" character, or this is "true" of the passions and actions ascribed to human life as depicted by the author; we may even say that we "understand" what a person does, feels, and thinks and why he acts and thinks as he does, or that we have an "insight" into the complex causal structure of his mind and passions—but this kind of truth, understanding, and insight seems to belong exclusively to a single work, the unique experiences, people, and situations depicted in it, and the peculiar, subjective view of them taken by the author.

Thus there arises a specific meaning of truth and knowledge belonging exclusively to the aesthetic context itself. What is called "true" seems to belong only, or primarily, to the experiences, feelings, actions, and situations evoked by the literary work, or to the unique way of rendering these aspects of reality in the poetic creation. This is a primary meaning of truth ascribed to the literary discourse and analyzed by aesthetic theory. It is to be distinguished from a secondary meaning which is quite different and which does not apply to the literary work itself but to certain general inferences drawn from it. What makes the problem of truth in literature so confusing is the interplay of the two meanings; for the primary, or aesthetic, meaning does not correspond to the ordinary employment of the term, whereas the secondary, or inferential, meaning does. And it is usually this inferential kind of knowledge that we mean when we praise literature for its cognitive contribution; when we believe, and rightly so, that the literary portrait, despite its uniqueness and single-mindedness, yields insights into, or knowledge about, psychological and social processes explanatory of human behavior in general.

This is what Freud had in mind when he said that the poets "tend to *know* a great many things not yet dreamt of in our academic knowledge"; or Engels when he praised the greatness of Balzac, from whose portrait of French society, between 1816 and 1848, Engels claimed to "have learned more than from all the professional historians, economists, and statisticians of the period together." [3] When we apply the terms "truth" or "knowledge," in this sense, to literature, we mean that, in depicting the infinite variety, color, and texture of experience, the great passions of life, and the complexity of forces shaping the individual and society, the literary portrait also gives us a clue to causes and motivations, and insight into the mechanics and principles explaining the how and why, and a better understanding of, and orientation within, the fascinating and bewildering multiplicity of life. Thus it was assumed that the literary portrait of time provided certain clues, or insights, of this kind into the nature and function of significant aspects of experience and life; and this is a commonplace assumption. It is evident, however, that these so-called insights are generalizations, explanatory principles derived and *inferred* from the literary portrait; and that these general inferences deserve to be distinguished from the primary meaning of truth belonging to the aesthetic context itself.

The myth of Narcissus does not prove the psychological principle of narcissism; it shows it in operation. The case of Swann and Odette does not prove the sado-masochistic pattern of love; it shows it. Ivan Karamazov is not a demonstration of the conflict between generations, or the universal wish for parricide; he is an exhibit. *The Grapes of Wrath* is only secondarily a sociological study about the dust bowl and the tenant-farmer class in the South; primarily it is a portrait of a poor Oklahoma family in the process of migration and dissolution. *Anna Karenina* is only secondarily a psychological or social study; primarily and aesthetically, it is a magnificent portrait of a loveless marriage, a passionate adulterous love affair, and the tragic defeat of the two lovers.

This primary meaning is important for three reasons: first, it belongs exclusively to the literary, or poetic, context; second, it helps to explain how truth may be used as an attribute of reality and life itself—of events, experiences, feelings, and actions—and not only as a property of sentences, as it is in scientific discourse; and third, it suggests that literary truth contains an ineradicable element of subjectivity. In all these respects truth in literature differs from the ordinary employment of the term.

This difference manifests itself in several ways: (*a*) In the context of literature (or art) an aspect of experience may be called "true" as we speak of a true feeling, a true coin, a true friend, a genuine value in contrast to experiences and values which are said to be "false" and "artificial." Analogously (*b*) the term "true" may then be applied to the unique way in which these experiences and values are rendered and exhibited by the literary work. Thus aspects of life and reality may be said to be depicted "truly" in contrast to artistic expressions which are called false, maudlin, or *Kitsch*. In addition (*c*) it may also be asked whether or not a literary portrait elicits a "true" response, issues a "true" challenge to action, presents a "true" choice in the sense in which William James spoke of a "genuine option, forced, living, and momentous," [4] and in contrast to an appeal which may again be called "false," or simply flat, indifferent, and insignificant. This is what Rilke meant when he closed his poetic rendering of the "Archaic Torso Apollo" with the abrupt and lapidary injunction: "You must change your life." [5] Nothing is said, of course, as to how we will or should change our lives, only that a "true," or authentic, response should be forthcoming after being confronted with the statue, or the sonnet transcribing it into poetry. Finally (*d*) all three senses of "true" may then lead to ascribing the same attribute to the process of communication performed by the literary work. Aesthetic communication may be called "true" in the way in which we sometimes say that "true" communication is achieved when two people understand each other silently, in contrast to the failure in communication of people who talk past each other even though they employ sound and rational arguments.

What constitutes "truth" in these different senses falls into the subject matter of aesthetic theory and cannot be discussed here.[6] I have listed these four categories briefly in order to bring out the fact that truth, in this primary, aesthetic sense —similar, as we shall see, to the concept of truth in literary, or existentialist, types of philosophies—is quite different from what we ordinarily mean by the term. First, its meaning and criteria of verification belong primarily to the literary work itself; second, it recognizes a meaning of truth as an attribute of aspects of reality—true feelings, true choices, genuine values, authentic responses; and third, it involves an ineluctable and, at times, radical element of subjectivity. A negative instance, or failure of response, obviously does not invalidate it. What Wordsworth saw and felt at Tintern Abbey might not be seen and felt by any other visitor; what Proust experienced before going to sleep may never happen to others who are more fortunate in their sleeping habits; what Stephen Dedalus saw at Bella Cohen's was quite different from the visions appearing to his friends, and would have been totally incomprehensible to the mass of regular clients at the establishment. Yet all these visions and insights are thought to be "true" within the context of each work and for the characters depicted and the feelings evoked.

We have distinguished, first, an ordinary sense of literary truth: reports, observations, and statements of an empirical, descriptive nature; second, a primary sense of truth in literature belonging exclusively to the context of the work of art and eliciting ineradicably subjective responses. In what other sense do we recognize literary statements as legitimate sources of knowledge? How does the primary meaning of truth in literature give rise to a secondary and derived one, with which it is often confused? This transition, I think, involves several steps.

1. The literary portrait conveys knowledge by rendering and exhibiting significant aspects of experience and life which may not be "known" previously. Great writers and poets *are*, as Zola thought, sensitive observers painstakingly recording and carefully analyzing what goes on in the world and in their own souls; but they are more. They also invent or "make" *new* facts of life. The manifold of experience, its unique sensuous and emotional colors, tones, and values often assume the shape and "reality" they have only by virtue of the shape they are given in the literary expression. New aspects of experience and life come into existence in and through the work of poetic creation. And this enlarges the scope of what Russell once called our knowledge by acquaintance; that is, by acquaintance with things which did not exist for us until they were expressed, or "known," in poetry. Poetry expands and enriches the scope of experience, or the world of possible experience, accessible to man.

2. So far as the passions, thoughts, and actions of our own lives are concerned, this cognitive contribution of literature, by means of the truths exhibited in its own context, assumes an even greater significance. The literary portrait may convey knowledge by bringing into light and clarity what might otherwise have remained opaque and obscure within us.

Again, this is more than just using the poetic powers of intro-spection and self-analysis, though these be remarkable; for it is not only a matter of recording accurately what is there but of discovering what is there by finding the right expres-sion for it; and this ability is rarely given to nonpoetic observers and analysts of the human scene. Thus by seizing upon a "true" feeling and by rendering it "truly" in the unique literary expression, the poetic work often brings into life and consciousness what we may have felt and thought without "knowing" it.

There is nothing mystical about this process. It merely describes what everybody knows, namely, that the arts fulfill a function not duplicated by any other symbolic process in-vented by man; that poetry says things which cannot be said in any form of prose, however accurate, precise, and logical. It says them by showing them directly in the unique im-agery and creative expression which mark the great work of art, not by talking about what it shows. Hence, the arts also say much more than can be said about them by critics and philosophers, and are, in many respects, much more ef-fective in conveying what they have to say than other forms of discourse. For the adult human mind, like that of the child, is much more receptive to what is concretely shown and rendered pleasurably than to what is indirectly inferred and involves a process of abstraction from reality.

3. This specific function of literary works may then be transferred from the world of individual passions and ideas to the total structure of the self. We cognize what we are by re-cognizing ourselves and others in the literary portrait. The insights into the how and why, the causes and motivations of human conduct, originally expressed and validated within the context of the literary work itself, may now become in-sights into one's own self. By appreciating and understanding

the true creation of the literary portrait, we may also discover significant truths about the construction of our own being and lives. Thus does great art hold a mirror up to human nature. And thus are the frontiers of experience and self-knowledge extended by great literature, though its truths and insights may be confined to a single case representing a unique, qualitative rendering of life and reality.

In this act of self-recognition, however, we have already taken a step beyond the object of art as such. We have incorporated it into the world of our own experience; we have "generalized" at least to the extent that what was previously seen to be true within the aesthetic context is now also seen to be true within the context of our own lives. And once we have taken this step, it is easy to carry the process of generalization further.

4. When we do so (and we often do), literary insights are used in the secondary meaning of truth distinguished above. They now function in a way approaching the ordinary, general meaning of knowledge. For we may take the literary portrait as a clue not only to our own being, or to that of others; we may also make inferences about human beings, and society, under conditions of varying generality. Freud was too modest: the poets, strictly speaking, don't "know" what they "show"—though what they disclose and express makes an invaluable contribution to our knowledge by acquaintance. But to say that we gain knowledge from poetic insights means that we translate the individual literary portrait, as Freud and others have done, into statements achieving a certain degree of generality and confirmable on other, nonliterary grounds. In short, we transcribe the literary discourse into a scientific discourse, even though this transcription may fall short of the model of knowledge in the exact sciences. Thus when we praise literature as a source of

knowledge and a great teacher, we may mean that the literary statement, though confined to a unique case of fiction, is a clue, key, or model—almost in the nature of a hypothesis —which, in conjunction with other observations and other sources of information, may be used as the basis for formulating abstract concepts and drawing general inferences. When we make generalizations of this kind on the basis of a single case or a unique situation depicted in a novel—say Proust's treatment of time or Tolstoi's treatment of love and marriage—and claim that the novel is "characteristic" or "typical," we mean that the single case has served as a clue for a general hypothesis about these aspects of human life, that we have incorporated it into the sum total of our own experience, or that we have correlated it with observation and information gained from other, nonliterary sources. This, I think, is an empirical explanation of Hegel's correct observation that art exhibits the universal idea, or type, in the particular.[7] Thus the discovery of unconscious motivation is undoubtedly an "insight" of this kind, which is easily translated into a general scientific category. There are a great many such insights, or inferences—yielding general principles, psychological and sociological, which are useful for explanation and even prediction, at varying degrees of generality—that can be extracted from literary works. In this respect, great works of literature make an invaluable contribution to human knowledge.

For the most part, these inferences do not have the power of explanation and prediction expected from a body of scientific knowledge. This is an important restriction, but it must not be overstated. In the first place, the general body of knowledge in the human sciences is subject to the same limitations. Whatever may have been the hopes and claims of the pioneers in the eighteenth and nineteenth centuries, and whatever may be the future achievements of these sciences, there is little doubt today that they also fall short, far short, of the model of knowledge set by an advanced science like physics; and there is at least *reasonable* doubt that they will ever come anywhere near meeting the standards and matching the achievements of the exact sciences. In the second place, a literary analysis still seems to yield insights superior and inaccessible to the academic historian, sociologist, and psychologist. The "facts" which the poets deal with, or bring into life, do not always lend themselves to the objective methods of verification, experimental tests, and intellectual, conceptual manipulation characteristic of scientific knowledge. Or, when they are submitted to these methods, that which is valuable—cognitively valuable—in the literary insights is buried and lost. The significant aspects of human life, unfortunately, do not manifest themselves in a community of white rats. Or the human and social "truths" that are safest and soundest from a scientific point of view are often the most trivial and uninteresting; they rarely seem to have anything to say about those aspects of our lives which concern us most, or which we would most like to know. This raises an awkward problem of methodology.[8]

The qualities of time and their relationship to the self which we have discussed were literary "insights" into significant aspects of life and experience. I have insisted throughout that they are exhibited in the literary works themselves and that their function and significance must be seen and appreciated within the specific context and individual structure of the works discussed. Thus what is meant by these temporal qualities is shown by the original way in which these works articulate certain aspects of experience within the aesthetic context. Literary works show directly how the qualities of time function and operate in the lives and experiences of the characters. The "truth" of these qualities, therefore, is first exhibited and realized within the specific aesthetic context.

In addition, however, our analysis was also an attempt to generalize from the aspects of time disclosed by the literary work and the significance attributed to them. In other words, subjective relativity, duration, dynamic interpenetration, continuity, identity, eternity, transitoriness, or the fore-knowledge of death are descriptions which translate into abstract language what the literary portrait depicts and explicates in the specific case and concrete situation. They are abstract concepts about certain qualitative aspects of time in human experience which do not find a place in the construction of an axiomatic system of time in nature.

What degree of generality is to be attributed to them is not easy to say. The truth of subjective relativity is almost trivial. It seems to be universally confirmed in human experience, and is easily corroborated by objective psychological tests. That time manifests itself in human experience under the aspect of change, mutability, and transitoriness is another truism. That the direction of time in human experience is determined by the prospect of death appears to be another safe generalization. But whether the temporal succession of moments in experience discloses a legitimate meaning of eternity; or whether time in experience has the qualities of duration, continuity, and identity within the structure of the self is much more difficult to say. There is no doubt that literary works, and insights, have frequently shown these qualities and their significance in human lives; no doubt that duration, dynamic fusion, continuity, and identity are often depicted as strictly correlative aspects of time, self, and the structures of the literary work itself. But it cannot be said, with the same degree of assurance, that these notions are, or can be, corroborated and clarified within other contexts, i.e., by logical analysis or by the body of experience and related knowledge which different people bring to the literary portrait. What "illuminates" (in Jaspers' terms) one person's world of experience strikes another as strange and fanciful. There are limits to the degree of confirmability in the employment of these concepts; there are areas of vagueness and imprecision. It is easy to raise logical objections, or to cite negative instances, but this is invariably true of generalizations about human nature and conduct.

These limitations are reinforced when we ask what value, or significance, is to be assigned to these aspects of time. It is easy enough to say, on the basis of the literary evidence, in conjunction with other sources of information, that time has become a matter of increasing concern and anxiety in the modern world. We may then ask why this is so; and I have tried to deal with this question at some length, suggesting several explanations: disappearance of the medieval dimension of eternity; confinement of time to secular history; the failure of unified theories of history justifying a belief in teleology; the fragmentization of time in history and human experience, and its effects upon the self; and the increasingly instrumental value assigned to these fragments of time and the self. No doubt the literary preoccupation with the subject of time is felt to correspond to personal experience; no doubt it issues a challenge and elicits a response in the life of modern man. How general this response is; what aspects of time are more or less crucial, and for whom; what the respective weight is of the different factors responsible for this increasing awareness of time in our lives—these and other questions are again suffused by undeniable, and perhaps undesirable, elements of vagueness and imprecision. Not all subjects, as Aristotle observed wisely, lend themselves to the same degree of precision and accuracy.

Even less can be said in the normative sense, i.e., in the sense of generalizing as to what significance these aspects of time, and their relationship to the self, *should* have for the individual. We may recognize that certain temporal qualities like duration, continuity, eternity, or progression toward death are particularly significant in our culture; but this does not enable us to say much about what significance they ought to have in our lives. We may, for example, be able to appreciate the significance, and acknowledge the relative truth, of both the optimistic and the pessimistic human reaction to the inexorable march of time toward death—without identifying ourselves with either. Or we may acknowledge that art, in a special sense, discloses "eternal" essences, without finding them particularly exciting in terms of our own lives.

Similarly, Tolstoi exhibits in *Anna Karenina* significant aspects of love and marriage in and through the lives of Karenin, Anna, Vronsky, and Levin. These portraits, and the insights they yield into private lives, may be used as a key to certain generalizations about the nature of love and marriage in the nineteenth century. But they do not imply normative judgments. Tolstoi's portrait may be appreciated and recognized as "true" whether we envisage marriage as a religious sacrament or as a social convention; whether we are for or against divorce; and regardless of which side we take in judging the final tragedy. The most we can say, as in our discussion of time, is that the work issues a challenge to the reader and presents him with a "genuine option" to come to terms with the portrait exhibited by the artist and to orient himself in a world in which time, love, and marriage may have this significance. But it does not say what the option will be, must be, or ought to be.

Literature makes a moral appeal and may elicit a moral response; but it does not say, and cannot say, unless it be converted into a didactic, moral tract, what the response ought to be. Hence, it does not relieve us of the obligation and anguish of solving our own problems and of making our own choices with regard to the "eternal" themes of time, love, defeat, and death—even though it serves the perfectly legitimate, cognitive function of greatly enlarging the scope of experience available to us in making these choices. People who read for personal comfort are often disappointed by these nonmoral implications of literature; others who wish to reform man and society have turned into enemies and distorters of art. As a matter of fact, great literature (at least in its secular manifestations) is a salutary antidote against morality, a welcome relief from the pervasive, powerful, and constant pressure of moral systems upon human lives. To "know" how complex, manifold, and devious are the ways of mice and men, how infinitely colorful and ingeniously deceptive are the pages of the human comedy (including the footnotes of our own lives) may also give us a different outlook on life—a better understanding of the human situation. This orientation, as I have called it, is not necessarily the kind of knowledge which enables us to know what will happen, or what human beings will and ought to do. It is rather the familiar phenomenon of feeling more at home in the world, of gaining a better understanding of the ways of man,[9] though these ways be quite unpredictable.

Literary Philosophy

Literary types of philosophy transfer the method and function of literature into the domain of philosophy. They also translate what literature says in the "object language," i.e., in the objects of literary creation, into statements interpreting and generalizing from these literary symbols and images within the context of a rational, abstract discourse. These generalizations, however, or the rational discourse they construct, must always—as in the case of the literary treatment of time—be seen within the context of experiences significant to human existence. This type of philosophy, therefore, differs from the conception of philosophy as a science in several respects: (*a*) it has a different conception of the function of philosophy; (*b*) it deals with different themes and objects of knowledge; and (*c*) it uses different criteria of meaning and truth. I suggest that its primary cognitive function is analogous to the intellectual and emotional orientation within the world of private experience (characteristic of literature), in contrast to a rational reconstruction of a body of knowledge dealing with objective facts (characteristic of science).

The purpose of this type of philosophy is to clarify, or "illuminate," as Jaspers puts it, the conditions of human existence, not to explicate scientific concepts. The term "existentialism" is derived from this premise. "Existence," and "being," according to this conception of philosophy, designate modes of human life and experience; they do not refer to "being" in the sense of physical matter, or even in the sense of a metaphysical substance or substratum. Existence is invariably human existence; and the task of philosophy is essentially that of making the presuppositions, modalities, and pervasive categories of subjective human existence explicit and intelligible, not of validating or explicating the presuppositions and basic concepts of science. "All philosophical problems revert back to the problem of existence." [10] "Philosophy is the path of man who, historically situated in his time, seeks to understand being." [11] And "what being is for us [is] inseparable from what we ourselves are." [12] The point of departure for philosophy, therefore, is either a radical subjectivity, in the Cartesian tradition, or a mixed state in which objective and subjective modes of being—"being that surrounds us" and "being that we are" [13]—are indissolubly fused in immediate experience. This is the premise for all varieties of phenomenalism and existentialism. Science is believed to depart from, and distort, this basic premise. Hence the knowledge it conveys, though *objectively valid*, does not deal with the kind of truth which is of *primary concern* in the context of human lives.

Man is "historically situated"; or "we live in a temporal existence"; [14] hence, time becomes a crucial concept for this type of philosophy, as it does for literature. "It was the analysis of the notion of time," Bergson wrote, "which overturned all my ideas . . . and brought me to reject almost all of what I had hitherto accepted and to change my point of view completely." This startling reorientation referred, as we have seen, to Bergson's discovery that the concept of physical time discarded what he believed to be the most essential qualities of time in experience, and their relationship to man. And it is this notion of time, time as experienced and lived, which enters into all varieties of existentialism. From birth to death, human existence, self-conscious human existence, unfolds and manifests itself under the two conditions of temporality and of man's foreknowledge of death. That is the leitmotiv of Heidegger's *Sein und Zeit*. All existentialist thinkers assign to the category of time a central place in their metaphysical systems; all of them engage in a phenomenological analysis of the experiential qualities of time, not in a logical analysis of scientific concepts. Time is the essence only insofar as its qualities are subjectively significant, not insofar as its properties may refer to an objective structure in nature. The point of departure is the temporality, or historicity, of man's existence; the point of arrival is usually an attempt, whether in religious or nonreligious varieties of existentialism, to pass beyond, i.e., "transcend," this temporally situated mode of man's existence. This is one important link between this type of philosophy and literature.

There are others. Several years ago (1947), Karl Jaspers—probably more of an expert in the natural and social sciences than most existential philosophers—published a work called *Of Truth*, the first volume of a *Philosophical Logic*, a book of about eleven hundred pages. It is a strange work when compared with the texts of scientific logic as we know them in our classrooms. For it refers only once to the existence of formal logic, without discussing it; but it contains lengthy analyses of all sorts of topics, e.g., work, technology, bureaucracy, freedom, authority, God, *unio mystica*, the irrational, time, tragedy, love, and eternity, which would never find a place in ordinary texts of logic or epistemology. These are, of course, exactly the themes that have engaged literature throughout the ages. And if logic may be construed as an "illumination" of these value-charged aspects of human existence in history, then literature might also be said to have a "logic."

The close affinity between this type of philosophy and literature (or the arts) may also be shown by a brief reference to the degree to which they depend upon each other for mutual support. There are few poets, if any, who have ever drawn their inspiration from the *Weltanschauung* of the sciences. Lucretius is an exception; and perhaps Shelley—though, as Whitehead tried to show, Shelley recast and reinterpreted the scientific picture of the world to which he subscribed in a characteristically poetic, i.e., nonscientific, manner. Goethe's prolonged and frustrating quarrel with Newton was clearly inspired by an aesthetic view of the world which seemed incompatible with the world-view of science. Kierkegaard, Schopenhauer, Nietzsche, and Bergson are the pervasive philosophical influences upon contemporary literature, not Mach, Poincaré, Russell, or Carnap.

It is also quite instructive to look upon the matter from the other side, the relation of philosophy to literature. In the *Critique of Pure Reason*, Kant still thought of philosophy as a science; its primary task was to provide a rational justification of the presuppositions of science, i.e., Euclidean geometry and Newtonian physics. The subsequent *Critiques* sharply deviated from this approach to philosophy as a science. When Kant wrote the "metaphysical" foundations of morals, metaphysics was no longer a science; on the contrary, it was an inquiry into conditions of human experience (in morality or the arts) which were explicitly stated to lie beyond the domain of the sciences, whether natural or human. And it is this second, nonscientific meaning of metaphysics which inaugurated the idealist and existentialist tradition in modern thought. Post-Kantian idealists addressed themselves to the "logic" of human existence and history, not to a logic of science. Philosophy in Schelling is a variety of romantic poetry. Schopenhauer listened to music as the veiled expression of deepest metaphysical truths. Nietzsche began philosophizing with an essay on Greek tragedy. Kierkegaard was not only a gifted literary person himself but constantly relied upon evidence and support from the arts. All these men were connoisseurs of the arts, not (except possibly Nietzsche) experts and critics of the sciences.

Existentialism in our age is practically indistinguishable from literary trends and the arts. Heidegger has written about Hölderlin and Rilke as precursors substantiating his own existential analysis.[15] Jaspers' references in the work just mentioned are illuminating. Russell is cited once—by name; Carnap twice, Wittgenstein once; otherwise no notice is taken of any logician, past or present, influential in the field of symbolic logic and the logic of science—which would of course be a scandal if Jaspers' book were meant to be a text in scientific logic, which it is not. Per contra, literary references abound: the Greek tragic poets are cited sixteen times, Calderon fifteen times, Shakespeare thirteen times, Goethe fourteen times, Dostoevski five times; and they are invariably enlisted in support of philosophical "truths."

In France, philosophy has always been primarily a literary rather than a scientific discipline; and contemporary French existentialists go back not only to literary philosophers like Kierkegaard, Nietzsche, and Heidegger, but to the poets and writers themselves: Baudelaire, Rimbaud, Tolstoi, Dostoevski, Kafka, Faulkner, etc. Moreover, what is a "literary" and what is a "philosophical" form of expression is often indistinguishable. Thus Tolstoi's *Death of Ivan Ilyitch* may be read as a legitimate philosophical treatise. Kafka may be hailed as an exponent of both atheistic existentialism and dialectical theology. The novels and plays of Sartre, Marcel, and Camus are as genuine, or authentic, an expression of their "metaphysics" as their official philosophical texts and essays.

Finally, the concept of truth employed by this type of philosophy closely resembles the meaning of truth characteristic of the literary discourse. There is an ineluctable element of subjectivity in existentialist "truths," even when they represent inferences believed to be valid for the human condition in general. For they are inseparable from a private, personal response and "commitment"; and if this response fails to be forthcoming, these philosophies can only appeal to a renewed and more intensive search of one's own consciousness; they cannot, and do not, provide any objective criteria by which these truths could be tested and measured. Truth, then, is a subjective, not an objective phenomenon.

In addition, truth is only secondarily a property of sentences or statements. Primarily, it is an attribute of experience and existence, temporal existence. "We live in a temporal existence: truth is our path." [16] Jaspers does not mean, as a scientific philosopher might, that truth is never a finished product because every statement believed to be true is only a probable approximation. He means that truth in this scientific, descriptive sense is secondary. The primary truth is "human" truth, an attribute of the different "stages on life's path" (Kierkegaard), varying not only with the human and historical situation, not only with the growth of self-consciousness and self-knowledge, but also with the individual's response and commitment to the "truth." It "grows out of the union of thinking and living";[17] it is a confession: "The radical difference in the meaning of truth is indicated by the difference between the kind of truth, the validity of which does not concern my nature [*Wesen*], which reason acknowledges, but which it would be meaningless to confess, and the kind of truth which exists only because my life is commensurate with it, which I 'confess' when it is my truth and which vanishes with the failure to confess it." [18] Truth as defined in the context of science may be "necessarily valid"; but it is "by no means the kind of truth for which it would be meaningful to die. For this truth is independent of what I do and am. Philosophical truth, on the other hand, is not independent of myself, but *is valid only in so far as it is alive within me, because I am the truth*, in so far as I participate in ideas and realize the truth in existence . . ." [19]

This is, of course, philosophical theory going beyond the boundaries of literature. But I think it is worth noting that this kind of philosophical truth is not only a secular restatement of truth in the religious sense: "I am the truth." It also resembles the primary meaning of truth emerging within the context of literature (or the arts). Existentialist writers have introduced the term "authentic," in place of "true," as more appropriate to designate this "human" meaning of truth in the primary sense. But they employ the term in exactly the same way that "truth" may be applied to the aesthetic context; that is, referring to (*a*) a true (authentic) experience or form of existence, (*b*) a true (authentic) rendering of aspects of life, (*c*) a true (authentic) response, choice, or commitment (James's "genuine option"), and (*d*) a true (authentic) process of communication. All these senses of truth differ from the ordinary employment of the term, and resemble the primary meaning of truth in literature.

Literary philosophies proceed on the assumption that it is possible to provide some sort of cognitive orientation within the domain of value-charged, significant aspects of human experience and existence. I shall not discuss the questions of whether these types of philosophy make a worthwhile contribution to the task to which they address themselves, or to what extent they trespass upon, distort, or expand the legitimate field of the human sciences, or what metaphysical conclusions, if any, may be justified on the basis of this type of analysis. These are interesting questions; but they go far beyond the scope of this essay. I believe that what these philosophies do is wrongly called "metaphysics," as this term is derived from Aristotle's reflections on "first philosophy." They are not concerned with what there is in the world, that is, with a rational reconstruction of the most general, pervasive, and objective categories of "being" as they may be ascribed to the world of nature. Instead, they deal with the question, "what is man?" (that Thou art mindful of him); that is, with an attempt to render intelligible the significant aspects of human experience and existence. Hence they have close ties not only with the arts but also with religion. Some

of them are religious throughout; others, accepting Zara-
thustra's message that God is dead, are atheistic. But whether
religious or not, they address themselves invariably to an
"illumination" of the human condition. They are varieties of
"metapsychology" rather than metaphysics in the Aristotelian
sense. And if they do make a contribution, I suggest that it
is in the direction of providing an orientation within the
value-charged dimension of experience and existence. This
may be considered a rational enterprise of cognitive value in
the sense in which literature was said to make a cognitive
contribution—even though this orientation, or "understanding," falls short, to varying degrees, of the model of "knowledge" as constructed in the context of scientific discourse.[20]

A similar trend, or dichotomy, may be observed in the
work of a philosopher who does not belong to what I have
called the literary tradition in modern thought. Whitehead
came from a background of formal logic and the philosophy
of science, before he turned to "metaphysics" in the traditional, nonscientific sense. Yet this turning toward metaphysical speculation came about, if we are to believe his own
words, primarily as a result of his reading poetry, more specifically, romantic poetry. "It is in literature that the *concrete outlook* of humanity receives its expression," he wrote
in the chapter called "The Romantic Reaction" in *Science
and the Modern World*.[21] Again, this reversal from philosophy conceived as science is due to aesthetic influences.
Science presents a rational reconstruction of the world, alien-
ated or divorced from the reality and value characteristic of
the human, experiential response to nature and history. "Remembering the poetic rendering of our concrete experience,
we see at once that the element of value . . . must not be
omitted in any account of an event as the most concrete
actual something. . . . Value is an element which permeates

through and through the poetic view of nature. We have only to transfer to the very texture of realization in itself that value which we recognize so readily in terms of human life. This is the secret of Wordsworth's worship of nature." [22]

In other words, the poets convey the meaning of "concrete experience"; moreover, the clue to these value-charged, significant aspects of experience lies in the values which we recognize "in terms of human life." "Thus we gain from the poets [not the scientists] the doctrine that a philosophy of nature must concern itself at least with these five [*sic*] notions: change, value, eternal objects, endurance, organism, interfusion." [23] Change, significance, eternal objects, endurance, interfusion, are aspects of experience all of which were characteristic of the literary treatment of time. If the approach to philosophy is modeled after an aesthetic outlook on life, "it follows that philosophy is not a science." [24] To say that philosophy is not a science, of course, is not to say that it cannot include or account for science. Whitehead has always dealt with the logic and place of science in the modern world; and this distinguishes him from what I have called the literary tradition in philosophy.

What he shares with literary philosophers is the belief that the task of philosophy consists not only in explicating the logic of science but also in reversing the process of logical abstraction for the purpose of returning, if possible, to the concrete qualitative aspects of life fused in immediate experience. Whitehead has been fully alive to the intellectual contribution made by formal logic: "The process of human thought is derived from the progressive enlightenment produced thereby" [i.e., logical analysis].[25] But he also believed that "the task of philosophy is to reverse this process [of logical abstraction] and thus to exhibit the fusion of analysis with actuality." [26] And for this task "logic conceived as an

adequate analysis of the advance of thought is a fake." [27]
"Actuality" is also described in such terms as the "concrete
unity of experience," or "a feeling for nature as exhibiting
entwined prehensive unities, each suffused with modal presences of others." [28]

Now this language obviously belongs to a literary, not to
a scientific, discourse. It is language appropriate for commenting upon the first book of Wordsworth's *Prelude;* and
despite its technical vocabulary, it is the kind of language
which we have repeatedly encountered in the literary treatment of time. Some unitary, unifying quality is exhibited in
the succession of temporal moments, some quality of continuity and endurance. These qualities are "entwined"; they are
"unities of interpenetration," in Bergson's language; they do
not succeed each other serially, but are dynamically interrelated and fused—"suffused with modal presences of others,"
i.e., with colors, tones, and values embedded in the texture of
immediate experience. Thus it is again the aspects of duration, flow, continuity, unity, and the dynamic fusion of
events in time which emerge as concrete qualities of experience and which are permeated with value and significance.
These qualities are said to be "exhibited," as a work of art exhibits what it has to say. And the whole process, or task of
philosophical reconstruction, is said to convey a "feeling
of nature," a strange way of describing the end product of
knowledge in the ordinary sense, but a perfectly familiar and
legitimate way of describing the cognitive function of literature. And "what is the evidence," Whitehead asks, for this
philosophical, or nonscientific reconstruction of the world
of experience? "The only answer is the reaction of *our own
nature to the general aspects of life* in the universe." [29] This
formulation comes close to the language of literary and existentialist thinkers, suggesting as it does that the process of

verification is not simply a matter of objective methods and intellectual operations but invariably involves a reference to our own nature, the unique, total structure of the self, ineluctably subjective and personal.

In a general and roundabout way we have returned to our point of departure. The philosophical problem of time, we observed then,[30] originates in the peculiar dilemma between what seems psychologically most certain and significant, on one side, and what is logically clear and meaningful, on the other. The subjective components of time in human experience lead to ambiguities and contradictions when tested critically. The logically pure concepts of time eliminate those aspects of time which seem to be immediately given and which are of deep concern to the span of human life. Thus orientation within the river of time and life—the "thoughts, knowledge, poetry, music, love, friendship, hates, passions" of which, for Tolstoi, "real life" is compounded [31]—seems to be most incompatible with a scientific reconstruction of the world. The more we tend to realize an ideal of knowledge modeled after the exact sciences, the more we tend to lose a basis for orienting ourselves intelligently and significantly within the diffuse experiential context of our lives. The dilemma may not be absolute; but it undoubtedly reflects a polarization, to varying degrees, of human thought in general. To the extent to which thought moves in the direction of scientific knowledge, it moves away from the grounds and conditions of "real life" as Tolstoi and other poets envisaged them; to the extent to which the human mind attempts an orientation within the value-charged aspects of time and life, it moves in the direction of art and literature.

NOTES

Chapter One

[1] Ernst Cassirer, *An Essay on Man* (New York: Doubleday, 1953), p. 72.

[2] Cf. Morton G. White, *Social Thought in America* (New York: Viking, 1949), p. 12 for a similar definition of historicism as characteristic of five eminent social thinkers in America. For a distinction between metaphysical and methodological historicism, see chap. iv, below.

[3] Thomas Mann, *The Magic Mountain* (New York: Knopf, 1949), p. 541.

[4] Wyndham Lewis, *Time and Western Man* (New York: Harcourt, 1928).

[5] Hans Reichenbach, *The Rise of Scientific Philosophy* (Berkeley and Los Angeles: University of California Press, 1951), p. 144.

[6] St. Augustine, *Confessions*, Bk. XI.

[7] Cited by Madeleine B. Stern, "Counterclockwise: Flux of Time in Literature," *The Sewanee Review*, XLIV (1936), 338–365.

[8] Bertrand Russell, *Human Knowledge* (New York: Simon and Schuster, 1948), p. 267.

[9] Cited by M. F. Cleugh, *Time* (London: Methuen, 1937), p. 2.

[10] The "cultural relativity" of time is another aspect, not treated here, of the general preoccupation with time in modern thought—in addition to the importance of the problem in physics, metaphysics, and literature. Cf. Benjamin Lee Whorf, *Collected Papers on Metalinguistics* (Washington, D.C.: Department of State, 1952) and Ernst Cassirer, *The Philosophy of Symbolic Forms*, Vol. I—Language (New Haven: Yale University Press, 1953).

[11] John E. Boodin, *Time and Reality* (New York: Macmillan, 1904), p. 65; cited by M. F. Cleugh, *op. cit.*, p. 10.
[12] St. Augustine, *op. cit.*
[13] Bertrand Russell, *op. cit.*, p. 212.
[14] Ralph Barton Perry, *The Thought and Character of William James* (Boston: Little, 1935), Vol. II, p. 623.

Chapter Two

[1] These subdivisions are taken from the work of Hans Reichenbach; cf. *Philosophie der Raum-Zeitlehre* (Berlin-Leipzig: W. de Gruyter, 1928; an English translation is in preparation); *Atom and Cosmos* (New York: Macmillan, 1933), chap. iii; and *The Rise of Scientific Philosophy* (Berkeley and Los Angeles: University of California Press, 1951), chap. ix. The term "coördinative definition" is also Mr. Reichenbach's.
[2] Thomas Mann, *op. cit.*, p. 66.
[3] Quoted by André Maurois, *Proust: Portrait of a Genius* (New York: Harper, 1951), p. 158.
[4] Virginia Woolf, *Orlando* (New York: Harcourt, 1928), cited by Madeleine B. Stern, *op. cit.*, p. 351.
[5] Cf. Bertrand Russell, *Principles of Mathematics* (2d ed.; London: G. Allen, 1937), Part V: Infinity and Continuity; and *Our Knowledge of the External World* (New York: Norton, 1929), chaps. v, vi, vii.
[6] The following groups of quotations are from Heraclitus, Omar Khayyám, Thomas Wolfe, and James Joyce, and again Wolfe, in that order.
[7] Johann W. Goethe, "Dauer im Wechsel" in the series of poems called *Gott und Welt.*
[8] Virginia Woolf, *To the Lighthouse* (New York: Random House, 1937), p. 158.
[9] Thomas Wolfe, *Look Homeward, Angel* (New York: Random House, 1934), p. 192; cited by Margaret Church, "Thomas Wolfe: Dark Time," *Publications of the Modern Language Association,* LXIV (Sept., 1949), 629–638.
[10] William James, *Principles of Psychology* (New York: Holt, 1899), I, chap. 17; James's whole chapter on "Time" is still very much worth reading.
[11] Hans Reichenbach, *The Rise of Scientific Philosophy*, pp. 148–149.
[12] Hans Reichenbach, "Les Fondements Logiques de la Méchanique des Quanta," *Annales de l'Institute Henri Poincaré* (1953), pp. 155–156.
[13] The analogy between the mind and geological or archaeological stratification occurs in Marcel Proust, *Remembrance of Things Past* (New York: Random House, 1934), I, 143; and in Freud's eloquent description at the beginning of *Civilization and Its Discontents* (3d ed.; London: Hogarth Press & Inst. of Psychoanalysis, 1946), pp. 15 ff. Geology and

archaeology were, of course, characteristic "temporal" sciences developed in the nineteenth century.

[14] Joseph G. Brennan, *Thomas Mann's World* (New York: Columbia University Press, 1942), p. 142.

[15] Jean Pouillon, *Temps et Roman* (Paris: Gallimard, 1946), Part II, chaps. 1 and 2 entitled *Les Romans de la Durée.*

[16] Cited by Madeleine B. Stern, *op. cit.,* p. 347. (Italics mine.)

[17] Cf. title of M. Heidegger's *Sein und Zeit* (6th ed.; Tübingen: Neomarius, 1949); the subtitle of Part I which, after the introduction, constitutes the whole of this volume (Part II, which was to be a second volume, has never been published) makes this point still more explicitly. It reads: "The interpretation of *Dasein* on the basis of temporality and the explication of time as the transcendental horizon of the question about *Sein.*"

[18] In this respect it differs from the previous discussion based upon the contrast between time in experience and time in nature.

[19] A recent detailed analysis of the fallacies involved in the notion of a substantial self may be found in Gilbert Ryle's *The Concept of Mind* (London: Hutchinson's, 1949). Mr. Ryle, I think, is unduly concerned with Descartes as the bête noire. Descartes only produced a sophisticated version of the general belief predominantly held in the West down to the present.

[20] For a nontechnical account of the Buddhist doctrine of the self as composed of various "bundles" (skandhas) analogous to Hume's analysis, cf. F. Harold Smith, *The Buddhist Way of Life* (London: Hutchinson's, 1951), pp. 46 ff.; and Christmas Humphreys, *Buddhism* (Harmondsworth, Middlesex, England: Penguin Books, 1951), pp. 87 ff., 95 ff., 119, *passim.* This small, inexpensive volume also contains an excellent bibliography referring to more technical studies of the various aspects of Buddhism, including the doctrine of the self.

[21] (New York: Avon Publications, Inc., 1952), p. 124.

[22] (New York and London: Harper, 1945), p. 37.

[23] David Hume, *A Treatise of Human Nature,* ed. by L. A. Selby-Bigge (Oxford: Clarendon, 1888), Bk. I, Section VI: *Of Personal Identity.* The passages cited are from pp. 252, 253, 259. Italics in the last quote are mine.

[24] *Ibid.,* p. 261.

[25] The term "ego psychology" is primarily used in psychoanalytic literature; cf. Anna Freud, *The Ego and the Mechanism of Defense* (New York: Norton, 1946) or Otto Fenichel, *The Psychoanalytic Theory of Neurosis* (New York: Norton, 1945), pp. 463 ff. The phrase "dynamic and economical organization" used in the text is Fenichel's, *ibid.,* p. 466. I must again emphasize, however, that I do not pretend to give a psychological analysis of the ego. That would be impossible within the scope of this essay. I have introduced the two conditions, the principles of dynamic organization and temporal continuity, as minimum conditions for what is known as personal identity in experience (neglected by an analysis such as Hume's) and in order to show in what sense and by what means the literary portrait (as in Proust, for example) makes a contribution to these aspects of the self by its analysis of time. For a discussion of these conditions in a generalized psychological theory of personality, see Gardner Murphy, *Personality* (New York and London: Harper, 1947), Part IV.

[26] Immanuel Kant, *Critique of Pure Reason*, tr. by Norman Kemp Smith (London: Macmillan, 1933), pp. 131 ff.

[27] David Hume, *op. cit.*, p. 252.

[28] Sir Charles Sherrington, *Man on His Nature* (New York: Doubleday, 1953), p. 222.

[29] The term "symbolic reference" is from Joseph Frank's essay, "Spatial Form in the Modern Novel," reprinted in John W. Aldridge, ed., *Critiques and Essays on Modern Fiction, 1920–1951* (New York: Ronald Press, 1952), p. 46. Mr. Frank also uses terms like "reflexive reference" or "reflexive relations." I do not share Mr. Frank's thesis that this use of time by certain writers is a way of introducing space as the basic form into the modern novel.

[30] *Ibid.*, p. 45.

[31] David Daiches, "Virginia Woolf," in John W. Aldridge, ed., *op. cit.*, p. 492. Mr. Daiches' essay contains an excellent diagrammatic analysis of Virginia Woolf's concept of time in *Mrs. Dalloway*. The essays by Daiches and Frank are very perceptive detailed studies of the meaning of time in Virginia Woolf, Joyce, Proust, and Djuna Barnes. They fail, in my opinion, to recognize the importance of the distinction between physical and psychological time—though Mr. Daiches discusses, as Mr. Frank does not, the correlation between the structure of psychological time and the structure of the self. Cf. also Mr. Daiches' study, *Virginia Woolf* (Norfolk: New Directions, 1942).

[32] J. W. Goethe, *op. cit.*; the passage reads in German: "Lass den Anfang mit dem Ende sich in Eins zusammenziehn"; and is related to another Goethe maxim, cited below, n. 52: "Der ist der glücklichste Mensch, der das Ende seines Lebens mit dem Anfang in Verbindung setzen kann," from *Maximen und Reflexionen*, Part II. The last two lines of Goethe's Orphic *Urworte*, "Dämon," also fit into this context: "Und keine Zeit und keine Macht zerstückelt geprägte Form, die lebend sich entwickelt."

[33] Cf. Harry Levin, *James Joyce* (Norfolk: New Directions, 1941), Part III, chap. i: "The Nightmare of History."

[34] Thomas Wolfe, *The Story of a Novel*, reprinted in *Only the Dead Know Brooklyn* (New York: New American Library, 1947), pp. 140–141. (Italics mine.)

[35] St. Augustine, *op. cit.*, Bk. X. (Italics mine.)

[36] Cf. Herbert J. Muller, *Thomas Wolfe* (Norfolk: New Directions, 1947) and Margaret Church, *op. cit.* above.

[37] Wolfe, *The Story of a Novel*, pp. 122–124. (Italics mine.)

[38] Cf. the recent volume of critical essays on Wolfe: Richard G. Walser, ed., *The Enigma of Thomas Wolfe* (Cambridge: Harvard University Press, 1953). I happen to think that Wolfe was more successful as an artist than seems to be the general opinion of more qualified literary critics.

[39] Cited by Georges Poulet, *Études Sur Le Temps Humain* (Paris: Plon, 1950), pp. 396–397.

[40] André Maurois, *op. cit.*, p. 158.

[41] *Ibid.*

[42] *Ibid.*, p. 159.

[43] Marcel Proust, *Remembrance of Things Past* (New York: Random House, 1927), I, 776.

⁴⁴ Cf. Fernand Vial, "Le Symbolisme Bergsonien Du Temps Dans L'Oeuvre De Proust," *Publication of the Modern Language Association*, LV (1940), 1191–1212; or Harry Slochower, "Marcel Proust: Revolt Against the Tyranny of Time," *The Sewanee Review*, LI (1943), 370–387; or the recent biography of Proust by André Maurois, cited above. Proust's theory of memory is developed from Henri Bergson's *Matter and Memory* (New York: Macmillan, 1911).

⁴⁵ See Jean Pouillon, *op. cit.*, p. 54.

⁴⁶ Cf. Immanuel Kant, *op. cit.*, pp. 149, 156, *passim.*

⁴⁷ Marcel Proust, *op. cit.*, II, 996.

⁴⁸ T. S. Eliot, "Burnt Norton," *Four Quartets* (New York: Harcourt, 1943), p. 5.

⁴⁹ *Op. cit.*, I, 143.

⁵⁰ *Op. cit.*, II, 1123. (Italics mine, because I think the phrase "no break of continuity" is crucial for Proust's conception of self-identity in contrast to Hume's.)

⁵¹ *Op. cit.*, II, 996.

⁵² Cf. above, n. 32.

⁵³ F. Scott Fitzgerald, *The Great Gatsby* (New York: Bantam Books, 1945), p. 106. Quoted by permission of Charles Scribner's Sons.

⁵⁴ *Ibid.*, p. 118.

"He [Fitzgerald] was haunted, as Malcolm Cowley has said, by time as if he wrote in a room full of clocks and calendars." Arthur Mizener, "F. Scott Fitzgerald: The Poet of Borrowed Time," in John W. Aldridge, ed., *op. cit.*, p. 287.

⁵⁵ Russell, commenting upon Shakespeare's

> "And yet to times in hope my verse shall stand
> Praising thy worth, despite his cruel hand,"

calls this belief of poets "that their own verses are indestructible" a "conventional literary conceit." Bertrand Russell, *A History of Western Philosophy* (New York: Simon and Schuster, 1945), p. 46.

⁵⁶ *Op. cit.*, I, 141, 143; II, 1001, where the phrase "unconscious self" occurs. Proust, of course, had a particularly keen sense for "unconscious" processes in human motivation and artistic creation.

⁵⁷ Sigmund Freud, "Das Unbewusste," in *Theoretische Schriften* (Vienna: Int. Psychoanalytischer Verlag, 1931), p. 121.

⁵⁸ Sigmund Freud, *New Introductory Lectures on Psychoanalysis* (New York: Norton, 1933), p. 104.

⁵⁹ The most interesting article is Marie Bonaparte's "Time and the Unconscious," *The International Journal of Psycho-Analysis*, XXI (Oct., 1940), 427–468. This paper discusses psychological, literary, and philosophical aspects of time, some of which coincide with and reinforce the basic arguments of the present study. Miss Bonaparte distinguishes three senses of "timelessness": (1) the unconscious has no knowledge of time; (2) the unconscious is completely unaffected by the process of time; (3) the unconscious does not perceive time. She concludes that (1) is a "truism"; (2), i.e., Freud's thesis in the text, must be qualified: "repressed psychic content undergoes *some* modification, however unalterable it may appear to our conscious minds"; and that (3) above "seems extremely likely"; *ibid.*, pp. 438–439. Miss Bonaparte also cites very good literary

material, and brings out the interesting point that Freud's own philosophical ideas on time closely followed Kant's, with the difference that Freud translated Kant's concept of a *synthetic* a priori form of intuition into the psychoanalytic terminology of projection; *ibid.*, pp. 466 ff. Cf. also Lucille Dooley, "The Concept of Time in Defense of Ego Integrity," *Psychiatry*, IV (1941); Sabina Spielrein, "Die Zeit im unterschwelligen Seelenleben," *Imago*, IX (1923); Paul Schilder, "Psychopathologie der Zeit," *Imago*, XXI (1935). Among nonanalytic psychologists, William James's *Psychology*, I, chap. 17 still remains an excellent account.

[60] W. T. Stace, *Religion and the Modern Mind* (New York: Lippincott, 1952), p. 243. For the vast literature on mysticism, cf. the same author's *Time and Eternity* (Princeton: Princeton University Press, 1952).

[61] E.g., in the works of Mr. Reichenbach cited above; or Harold F. Blum, *Time's Arrow and Evolution* (Princeton: Princeton University Press, 1951).

[62] Martin Heidegger, *op. cit.*, pp. 235 ff., where Heidegger quotes (p. 245) a medieval saying to the effect that "as soon as man is born, he is old enough to die."

[63] This distinction corresponds roughly to one by Pierre Janet, as cited by Marie Bonaparte, *op. cit.*, p. 454, who distinguished between a "creative" and a "destructive" aspect of time. In addition, however, Janet recognized a "conservative" aspect corresponding to the time of the historians.

[64] Thomas Mann in *This I Believe*, ed. by Edward R. Murrow (New York: Simon and Schuster, 1952).

[65] At least according to St. Augustine.

[66] Cf. *Timaeus*, 38 B.C.

[67] Cf. Max Weber, *The Protestant Ethic and the Spirit of Capitalism* (New York: Scribner, 1930); or R. H. Tawney, *Religion and the Rise of Capitalism* (New York: Harcourt, 1926).

[68] Johann W. Goethe, *Faust*, translated by Bayard Taylor (Boston and New York: Houghton Mifflin, 1924), I, 68. A literal translation of "there let, at once, my record end" (Taylor's version) is "then let time have a stop for me."

[69] *Ibid.*, II, 308.

[70] *Ibid.*, II, 295.

[71] *Ibid.*

[72] T. S. Eliot, *Collected Poems* (New York: Harcourt, 1934), p. 13.

[73] Machado de Assis, *Epitaph of a Small Winner* (New York: Noonday, 1952), p. 188.

[74] Cf. Charles Baudelaire, "L'Ennemi," "Le Gout du Néant," and "L'Horloge" in *Les Fleurs Du Mal*, tr. by C. F. MacIntyre (Berkeley and Los Angeles: University of California Press, 1947).

[75] Shakespeare's Sonnets, especially XII, XV, LXIV, LXV, are constant reminders of this melancholy theme.

[76] Percy Bysshe Shelley, "Mutability."

[77] Note how the quality of the inexorable, melancholy progression of time toward death, and the vanity of all human endeavors, is translated into the rhythm and the tonal quality of the poetry.

[78] Aldous Huxley, *After Many a Summer Dies the Swan*, pp. 122–123.

[79] Cf. Van Meter Ames, *Proust and Santayana: The Aesthetic Way of Life* (Chicago-New York: Willett, Clark, 1937).

[80] Proust, *op. cit.*, II, 996.

[81] T. S. Eliot, *Four Quartets*, p. 5.

[82] Marcel Proust, *op. cit.*, I, 777.

[83] André Maurois, *op. cit.*, p. 6.

[84] See Bertrand Russell, *Our Knowledge of the External World* (New York: Norton, 1929), p. 181.

[85] James Joyce, *Portrait of the Artist as a Young Man*, in the *Portable Joyce*, ed. by Harry Levin (New York: Viking, 1947), p. 518.

[86] Cf. Benjamin Lee Whorf, *op. cit.*, pp. 32–33.

[87] For an interesting discussion of the scientific merits of the organic conception of history, see H. Stuart Hughes, *Oswald Spengler* (New York: Scribner, 1952), especially chap. iii.

[88] Thomas Mann, *Freud und die Zukunft* (Vienna: Bermann-Fischer, 1936), p. 30, wherein the phrase "timeless schema," cited above, occurs in the same context.

[89] Goethe, *Faust*, II, 4–5.

[90] *Ibid.*, p. 313.

[91] Cited by Werner Jaeger in the introduction to *Gods and Heroes*, Myths and Epics of Ancient Greece (New York: Pantheon, 1946), p. 27.

Chapter Three

[1] Cf. above, chap. i, n. 4.

[2] Thomas Mann, *Freud und die Zukunft* (Vienna: Bermann-Fischer, 1936), pp. 14–15.

[3] Quoted by Lionel Trilling in "Psychoanalysis and Literature," *Horizon* (Sept., 1947).

[4] Sigmund Freud, *Der Wahn und die Träume in W. Jensen's "Gradiva"* (Gesammelte Schriften IX; Vienna: Int. Psychoanalytischer Verlag, 1925), pp. 274–364.

[5] Cf. Harry Levin, *James Joyce*, p. 90.

[6] St. Augustine, *The City of God* (London-New York: Everyman's Library, 1945), Bk. XII, chaps. 15, 16.

[7] Continuous creation, as well as its religious corollary, the doctrine of continuous grace, are fully discussed, with a great many interesting references, by Georges Poulet, *op. cit.*, introduction.

[8] David Hume, *op. cit.*, p. 261.

[9] Cf. above, chap. i, n. 2.

[10] Cf. Harold D. Lasswell and Abraham Kaplan, *Power and Society* (London: Routledge, 1952), p. xiv.

[11] John Dewey, *Logic, the Theory of Inquiry* (New York: Holt, 1938), p. 501. I am not citing any references to the enormous literature on the varieties of historicism here in this country and in Europe.

[12] E.g., in John Dewey, *Freedom and Culture* (New York: Putnam, 1938).

[13] Cf. his letters to Conrad Schmidt (Aug. 5, 1890), Franz Mehring

(July 13, 1893), Heinz Starkenburg (Jan. 25, 1894), in *Karl Marx: Selected Works* (London: Lawrence and Wishart, 1942), pp. 380 ff.

[14] Cf. Karl Popper, "The Poverty of Historicism," *Economica* (1944–45) and *The Open Society and Its Enemies* (Princeton: Princeton University Press, 1950); F. A. Hayek, *The Counter-Revolution of Science* (Glencoe, Ill.: Free Press, 1952).

[15] Thus, both Popper in his *Open Society* and J. P. Sartre in *L'Existentialisme est un Humanisme* reach the same conclusion that "although history has no meaning, we can give it a meaning." (Popper.)

[16] Philip Rahv, "The Myth and the Powerhouse," *Partisan Review* (Nov.-Dec., 1953), p. 642.

[17] Cf. Spengler's essay called "Pessimism" in *Reden und Aufsätze* (Munich, 1937); Ludwig Marcuse, "Über den Pessimismus," *Der Monat* (May, 1953), pp. 166–176. This is not to overlook the fact that many contemporary thinkers still cling to the belief in progress, despite (and often in ignorance of) the powerful criticism to which this belief has been subjected. The concept—like that of the substantial self—is still a pervasive and unconscious component of the general climate of opinion; the will to believe dies hard, in spite of the evidence against it.

[18] W. H. Auden, *Collected Poems* (New York: Random House, 1945), p. 271.

[19] Cf. Eliot, Huxley, and many other literary and philosophical writers who are returning to the religious and/or mystical dimension of eternity.

[20] I have not distinguished, for the purpose of this study, between Spengler and Toynbee. The latter, of course, clings to a salvation element in his cyclical theory, reminiscent of St. Augustine and not characteristic of Spengler. But my point was simply to show that some variety of cyclical theory depicting the growth and decline of societies seems to be the only theoretical frame of reference within which a unified theory of history can still be constructed, and that the significance of these theories derives largely from venturing upon such universal reconstruction. Insofar as Toynbee is an Augustinian, he reflects the shift toward an antisecular, religious form of historicism which includes the aspect of eternity.

[21] A personal note will serve to illustrate this point. I read the New York *Times,* which reaches Los Angeles three or four days after the date of publication. Most people seem to find it strange to read news which is several days *old.* My own experience has been that the lapse of time makes absolutely no difference so far as the news is concerned—except to be helpful in making a selection between what was actually newsworthy a few days ago and what was not.

[22] The theme is almost universal in contemporary literature; cf., for example, Hedwig Koch, *Das Generationsproblem in der Deutschen Dichtung der Gegenwart* (Langensalza: H. Beyer, 1930), or K. T. Wais, *Das Vater-Sohn Motiv in der Dichtung* (Berlin-Leipzig: W. de Gruyter, 1931).

[23] It is surprising, though, how far the literal language of the slave market has been carried into other social areas, even into the world of sports; cf. the *language* (and possibly the practices) in national sports like baseball where players are "bought," "sold," and "traded," and where the Supreme Court has only recently been called upon again to decide whether baseball is a sport or a business.

[24] Marx was one of the first writers to develop this transformation of

man as a result of modern industrial society—one aspect of the more general theme of the "alienation" of modern man. The same concept is widely recognized in contemporary social psychology. Chaplin presented a brilliant visual portrait of the individual as a productive unit in the assembly line in the film *Modern Times*. Whorf, *op. cit.*, pp. 39 ff., also discusses a number of interesting social and psychological implications of our linguistic conceptualization of time, among them "our prorata allocation of value to time" (time wages, rent, credit, interest, depreciation charges, and insurance premiums), our "emphasis on 'saving time,'" the "high valuation of 'speed,'" the aspects of "monotony" and "regularity" associated with this conceptualization of time, and certain behavioral effects like "carelessness" and "gesturing."

Chapter Four

[1] Emile Zola, *Le Roman Expérimental* (Paris: Charpentier, 1923), pp. 123–126.

[2] See Isaiah Berlin, *The Hedgehog and the Fox* (London: Weidenfeld & Nicolson, 1953).

[3] Friedrich Engels, letter to Margaret Harkness, April, 1888, reprinted in *Literature and Art* (New York: International Publishers, 1947), pp. 41–43.

[4] William James, "The Will to Believe," *The New World* (June, 1896). It still remains to be shown, I think, what a profound influence this essay has had on contemporary existentialist theology.

[5] Rainer Maria Rilke, *Der Neuen Gedichte Anderer Teil* (Leipzig: Insel Verlag, 1920).

[6] Cf. John Hospers, *The Meaning of Truth in the Arts* (Chapel Hill: University of North Carolina Press, 1948), for the general problem. Hospers also uses the expression "true to" as characteristic of literary truth.

[7] At times literature also creates "types," especially in the older comedy, such as the "typical" miser, or the "typical" old spinster; but these possibilities are soon exhausted, and when we now refer to a literary portrait as being a type, we usually mean that it is nothing but a type; in short, inferior as literature.

[8] The problem arises in connection with the scientific status of psychoanalysis. Another aspect of the same problem is whether history includes an aesthetic element, since it is also concerned with the reconstruction of concrete, unique situations; cf. Arnold Toynbee, *A Study of History*, abridged (New York: Oxford, 1947), p. 43 and Alan Bullock, "Die Aufgaben der Geschichtsschreibung: Historie und Metahistorie," *Der Monat* (Jan., 1954), p. 343, where the same point is made with explicit reference to Dostoevski, Shakespeare, and Proust.

[9] In the sense of the phrase, nothing human is alien, or the proverb, to understand all is to forgive all. "Understanding" is used in this way, and the same proverb is cited by Whitehead in his essay, "The Aims of

Education," recently reprinted (New York: New American Library, 1953), p. 14. I suggest that the controversy between "knowledge" (*Wissen*) and "understanding" (*Verstehen*), which has received a good deal of attention in modern sociological and psychological theory, may also be interpreted, as Max Weber did, as the difference between descriptions which are factual, general, value-neutral, and descriptions which are charged with value and "significance" and involve the reconstruction of "concrete reality," or an "understanding of the characteristic uniqueness of the reality in which we move." Cf. Max Weber, *The Methodology of the Social Sciences*, tr. by E. A. Shils and H. A. Finch (Glencoe, Ill.: Free Press, 1949), p. 72.

[10] Karl Jaspers, *Philosophie* (2d ed.; Berlin: Springer Verlag, 1948), p. v.

[11] *Ibid.*

[12] Karl Jaspers, *The Perennial Scope of Philosophy* (New York: Phil. Lib., 1949), p. 26.

[13] *Ibid.*, pp. 12–13.

[14] Karl Jaspers, *Von der Wahrheit* (Munich: Piper, 1947), p. 1.

[15] See Martin Heidegger, *Holzwege* (Frankfurt: Klostermann, 1950); especially the chapter called "Why Poets," pp. 248–295.

[16] Jaspers, *Von der Wahrheit*, p. 1.

[17] *Ibid.*, p. 2.

[18] *Ibid.*, p. 651.

[19] *Ibid.*, pp. 651–652. (Italics mine.)

[20] The term "orientation" also occurs frequently in existentialist writings; e.g., the first book of Jaspers' *Philosophie* is entitled "Philosophical World-Orientation."

[21] A. N. Whitehead, *Science and the Modern World* (Harmondsworth, Middlesex, England: Penguin Books, 1938), p. 93. (Italics mine.)

[22] *Ibid.*, p. 114.

[23] *Ibid.*, p. 107.

[24] A. N. Whitehead, "Mathematics and the Good," in *Essays in Science and Philosophy* (New York: Phil. Lib., 1947), p. 113.

[25] A. N. Whitehead, "Immortality," *ibid.*, p. 95.

[26] "Mathematics and the Good," *ibid.*, p. 113.

[27] "Immortality," *ibid.*, p. 96.

[28] Whitehead, *Science and the Modern World*, p. 103.

[29] "Immortality," *op. cit.*, p. 94. (Italics mine.)

[30] See pp. 5 ff. above.

[31] Isaiah Berlin, *op. cit.*, p. 20, citing Tolstoi. The phrase between dashes is stated in Mr. Berlin's words.

INDEX